Stoking the Fire of Hope:

Fioretti for Our Times

Hermann Schalück, ofm

Stoking the Fire of Hope:

Fioretti for Our Times

Hermann Schalück, ofm

Franciscan Institute Publications
St. Bonaventure University
St. Bonaventure, New York 14778

1997

©1997
Franciscan Institute Publications
St. Bonaventure University
St. Bonaventure, New York, 14778

ISBN 1-57659-133-6

Printed at
    BookMasters, Inc.
    Mansefield, Ohio

Table of Contents

Abbreviations

Biblical texts use the *New American Bible* abbreviations

Franciscan and Other Texts

I. Writings of St. Francis

Adm = Admonitions
EpAnt = Letter to St. Anthony
EpFid = Letter to all the Faithful
EpOrd = Letter to the Entire Order
LaudDei = Praises of the Most High God
RegB = Rule of 1223
RegNB = Rule of 1221
Sal Virt = Salutation to the Virtues
Test = Testament of St. Francis

II. Other Early Franciscan Sources

1 Cel = Celano, First Life of Francis
2 Cel = Celano, Second Life of Francis
3 Cel = Celano, Treatise on Miracles
CL = Legend of St. Clare
Fior = Little Flowers of St. Francis
Giano = Chronicle of Brother Jordan of Giano
2 LAg = Clare, Second Letter to Agnes of Bohemia
LM = Bonaventure, Major Life of Francis
LP = Legend of Perugia
SC = *Sacrum Commercium*
SP = Mirror of Perfection

III. Other Abbreviations

GC = General Constitutions (OFM 1985)
PG = Migne, *Patrologia Graeca*
SCh = *Sources Chrétiennes*

Foreword

In this book I present a series of texts which were written between 1985 and 1996. With a few exceptions their style recalls that of the *Fioretti*, an anonymous collection of texts from the fourteenth century about some events, tendencies, and even tensions in the early days of the Franciscan family, written down in poetic and symbolic language. Although the *Fioretti* do not represent a reliable, historic source of Franciscanism, they do form an important witness about the way of St. Francis and his first followers.

The narratives presented here attempt to draw, in a similar way, from subjective experiences and events within today's Franciscan family on several continents and in many cultures. In the form of picturesque and sometimes unusual language, frequently in metaphors and comparisons, they present to Francis's brothers and sisters today's problems and challenges—especially the necessity of inculturating the Good News in various cultures and sociopolitical systems—and the question of the meaning of the Franciscan heritage in contexts different from that of the Middle Ages. Service in the leadership of the Order has given me opportunity for many new and unexpected experiences.

The texts in this book are spontaneous writings about these experiences. They are sketches which, over the course of time, I circulated to a good number of Franciscan brothers and sisters. Many have encouraged me to publish them in a single volume.

For a better understanding of the background for these stories, I have added a short introduction for each text. The heartfelt conclusion which I have made in these years and which I want to transmit through these texts is this: The Franciscan life-style must be passionate, reflective, down-to-earth, and liberating. However, in order to avoid the danger of empty talk, of ideology and verbal critiques, all the followers of Francis and Clare need to ground their lives in service, living out more than ever their experiences of mystery, contemplation, beauty, music, drama, and poetry. This book's title evokes that type of service to the Lord of History.

I thank Father Anthony Carrozzo, OFM, and Franciscan Institute Publications of St. Bonaventure University for their readiness to publish this book. I am grateful to Friars Louis Antl, Oswald Gill, and Boniface Kruger who made the original

Foreword

translations into English. Thanks to Pat McCloskey, OFM, for preparing this book for publication and to Sandy Howison for proofreading the final draft.

I dedicate this book to the countless Sisters and Brothers in all the world—committed members of religious orders as well as many others—whom I have been able to meet. Their example in following Jesus and their passionate love for all God's people, especially the poor, have encouraged me. They are the real authors of these stories and initiatives.

Hermann Schalück, ofm
Easter 1997

Prologue

Francis to his Brothers and Sisters Today

An Open Letter for the Year 2000

Dear Brothers and Sisters,

The Lord give you his peace!

Only three years now separate the human race from the moment of passing into a new millennium. Almost 2000 years ago our Lord and Brother Jesus of Nazareth made his visible entrance into our history. That is why the year 2000 is for Christians everywhere an important moment of remembrance, but also one of new realization and of courageously beginning anew.

Together with the whole of Christianity in East and West, North and South, you will celebrate the Incarnation of our God into history and into the cosmos. You live in a time in which it seems to many people that everything is possible but nothing is reliable and sure. It is, then, my duty to give you courage and to point out to you that the Spirit of God is still blowing, that there still exist certainties for which it is worth living, that the future may be a good one, and that the Franciscan family, trusting in the Lord, is called to be a sign of a renewed Church and a reconciled world. Looking forward to the year 2000 then, I would like to present to all of you the following counsels and requests.

Be Signs of the God Who Promises Life and a Future

You are on the way with many brothers and sisters from all continents, cultures, races, and religious convictions, people who are insecure, skeptical, indifferent, or even desperate. Many are also simply cynical, homeless, disillusioned. Words, programs, projects, and loud appeals will not by themselves light the way into the new millennium. The world does not simply need teachers. It needs, above all, men and women, clerical and lay, who witness to a lived faith and a firm hope. It needs prophets and poets of a God who is present in the midst of history's lights and shadows, who wants life and a future for all, whose love makes no distinction between races and religions.

Fioretti for Our Times

Sister Clare and I have called this family into being so that it may be a sign of the living God, of a God who loves creation, especially what is small and insignificant in it. Therefore, your fraternities, communities, and families should be pre-eminently oases where God is experienced and adored, where his presence is celebrated in Word, Eucharist, and service to one another—oases of friendliness and peace. There the things must flourish which are always the most important: contemplation, prayer, liturgy, art, poetry, prophecy, music, and above all, love. May the spark of the divine be kindled anew in your hearts and in your houses, in your hermitages and universities, in schools, clinics, in the churches and simple chapels throughout the world. Be men and women who daily anchor your lives in the mystery of God and who are able to make a generous gift of God's goodness, mercy, and friendship, because you have experienced it personally.

To be sure, it is precisely in these last years that there has also spread among you a joylessness, tiredness, the crushing feeling of routine and uselessness. There are so many new, unsolved, and apparently insoluble questions and challenges for a life according to the Gospel. Although the times are complex and difficult, it is not good for a layer of gray ash to choke the living fire of joy in God and in the following of Jesus. How then is the Gospel still to shine out? How then are young people to join your communities? The best preparation for the year 2000, my brothers and sisters, is your conversion to the crucified and risen Lord, who has called you to manifest joy in the God of life and hope, trust in the Spirit and his holy operation. Only if you rediscover and live your passion for God can you render courageous service to the world, be prophets for a new epoch, and passionately defend others, especially the poor.

Living in Reconciled Differences

Pope John Paul II's letter *Tertio Millennio Adveniente* is an urgent call to conversion. The whole of Christianity in the first two millennia, says the pope, has not measured up to the task laid upon it by Jesus, to be for all people a visible sign of unity, love, and peace. At the threshold of the third millennium, therefore, all Christians are called to penance and to a greater faithfulness to the Lord's command.

Brothers and sisters of the Franciscan family, at the dawn of this new epoch you will render another important service to the Church if you begin by being reconciled to one another in your own hearts. I know that there is no longer any open hostility between the members of the one family. Many mutual prejudices of history have been overcome. Throughout the world there are now many beautiful forms of collaboration and communion within the one charism which Sister Clare and I have received from the Lord.

And yet much remains to be done. It is my desire that you should present more and more to the Church the vision of reconciled differences, without which there can be no ecumenism among Christian Churches, no dialogue among religions, no durable peace between races and peoples. I want you, clerics and lay, women and men, contemplatives in the world and contemplatives in enclosure, to meet everywhere, more than ever as equals before the one Lord. I admonish you to render to one another those acts of service without which there can be no true communion in the one Lord. Offer above all the service of prayer for one another, mutual information, help, counsel, spiritual assistance—including that of the sisters to the brothers—admonition, and positive example in the following of Jesus.

All brothers, clerics and lay, are always to keep close to their hearts my admonition to bestow special attention on the Sisters of St. Clare, without arrogance or paternalism. There should be deep respect for one another and true humility before the Spirit of the Lord, who works in everyone without distinction. Above all, give young people who ask about me and Clare the example of reconciliation and mutual edification. Is it not already time to perform together certain services whose efficiency and credibility depend on the solidarity of all—for example, the service of peace, justice, and the conservation of creation, the service of ecumenism and dialogue with the great non-Christian religions, service in the universities and academies of the Franciscan family? And could not your young brothers and sisters learn other people's languages much more than they have done up to now? To the extent that you come closer together, you will discover something of the universality of salvation, of the Church, and of the Gospel's dynamism in a torn and disturbed world.

Be Instruments of the Ongoing Creation, Witnesses of the Resurrection

Many of our contemporaries would like to have a detailed map for the way that lies ahead for the human family, with precise indications about paths, obstacles, distances and stages. Christians have no such maps for their way into the new millennium. But the "preferential option" for the crucified and risen Lord is their reliable compass. Anxieties and uncertainties may remain, but the compass gives us the confidence, indeed the certitude, that the direction is the right one. God the Lord has promised a good future for creation and for our history in the resurrection of his Son. For all of you, sisters and brothers of my family, I would, therefore, like to wish senses attentive to and a heart open for the co-responsibility which you bear for the world's future. In the tradition of the Jewish midrash, it is written:

> When God created the world
> He made all things a little incomplete:
> He did not make bread grow out of the earth, but only corn,
>   and how to bake bread we had to learn ourselves.
> Neither did God create bricks or even houses,
>   but only the clay of the earth.
> Bricks and houses are the work of people.
> God calls us to be collaborators in the creation of the world.
> People are called to continue and complete God's work.

You have only one planet, only a single air, only one water, a single surface of the earth. I remind you that you have to care for these as for your own brothers and sisters. Otherwise, they will no longer care for you. Tell your contemporaries they ought to apologize to Nature and to our Mother Earth for the damage done to them through indifference and egoism.

You will also be creative if you esteem what is small, poor, "minor," if you give a chance to the "smoking flax," allow the insignificant to signify, draw strength from stillness, distrust the big and loud word, prefer soft tones, believe in change through the Spirit of the Lord, and earnestly pray always for the Spirit of the Lord and his holy operation. You are creative if you believe in the possibility of conversion, of the gift of peace, of forgiveness. For this remains into the third millennium the task of the Lesser Brothers and Sisters, wherever they are—to bring together what is dispersed, to mend what is broken, to bind wounds, to give food for the hungry, to liberate the poor, to comfort the afflicted, to dry tears. In times both light and dark, your task remains this—to bake bread, to break bread, to share bread with the poor, to be bread for others. Where these wonders of change take place, there blows the Spirit of God, and the future is brought into being.

The Song of the Rainbow

I greet you from my heart. My wish for you is that the Lord of history may change your anxieties into hopes, your darknesses into light, your sadnesses into joyful anticipation. So I give you as a sign of my blessing a prayer for your journey:

Lord, make of us a rainbow,
  a visible sign of peace and reconciliation.
A rainbow which boldly bridges the two millennia,
  the old and the new.
A sign from heaven that you yourself have set there.
A sign of that promise which never deceives.
The rainbow is to be for everyone
  a sign of hope;
A sign of your love for creation,
  of the promise of your Spirit which renews the world.
Make us who follow you restless in a constructive way.
Make us restless, if we are too self-satisfied
  and too self-assured, too small, too narrow,
  if instead of remaining on the path we think
  ourselves already at the goal.
Make us restless if over the fullness of the things we possess
  we lose our thirst for your presence
  and for peace in justice.
As we look to the future, let us not manifest
  indifference and blindness,
  but neither blind zeal and restlessness.
Grant us the peace which comes from encountering you,
  the tact, friendliness, courtesy, amiability
  towards all life and towards non-living creatures, too.
Shake us awake, Lord, that we may be more daring,
  more in solidarity with one another,
  more attentive to your Word,
  more alert to hear the cry of the poor,
  more open to future generations.
May we follow you in greater faithfulness.
Yes, Lord, make us a rainbow,
a sign of hope for a new world.

Your Brother,

Francis of Assisi

Chapter 1
1985-1986

1985

1. On true and perfect joy

Background: At Pentecost in 1985, there was a general chapter of the Order. It was marked by lively debates about new directions and initiatives. The Holy See had appointed a special delegate for the chapter, which reelected the existing Minister General (John Vaughn) for a second term.

In the beautiful month of May 1985, Brother Francis of Santa Maria degli Angeli was coming back with Brother John of Santa Barbara from a six-year trip around the Order of Lesser Brothers. As they were coming up the Viale Giovanni XXIII toward the Portiuncula, Brother Francis said to Brother John: "Now I will tell you what true and perfect joy means. So please write this down.

"On our journey, we saw how many good, involved brothers there are, who follow the Gospel of our Lord Jesus Christ, live in close union with God, work hard, pursue old and new theology, live with the poor, and are servants and little people for the world and for the whole people of God. But write: This is not yet true joy.

"Now continue: The number of vocations has fortunately grown, new provinces have been founded and new novitiates as well as formation houses have been opened. The brothers have finally gone in where I myself could never go—into the heart of Africa. With a few exceptions, all the crises of the past twenty years have been resolved. Everywhere there has reigned unity in plurality and plurality in unity. But take note, John, that this too is not yet perfect joy.

"So write on: The brothers love the Church, the Lord Pope, the bishops and their own minister, but they also love the special favorites of God: the poor, the despised, the little people, and those robbed of their rights. Some of the brothers have in the last six years been persecuted and killed for their love of the Church. But even this, dear Brother John, is not yet perfect joy.

"So continue writing: As an Order, you have preserved sound traditions but you have also tried to read the signs of the new times. Almost all the brothers have understood my original views better. The Gospel life in brotherhood based on the *Regula Bullata* has, in accord with the Second Vatican Council, been brought back as a stable norm. Your Order's identity has been more clearly visible than for many centuries. Never have your brothers so carefully studied and investigated the things I said and wrote as in the last twenty years. Nowhere did I find authority crises arising from overstressing brotherhood. Where brotherhood is the norm, love and justice grow. Divisions are not to be feared; among the Franciscan families of women and men, I have almost always found respect, solidarity, and unity in essentials, as well as a common desire to follow the Gospel. All this has greatly edified and gladdened me. And yet, John, even this is far from perfect joy.

"Now write on as follows: You know, my brother, that I do not like to praise people, because all of us should glory only in the cross of our Lord Jesus Christ (Gal 6:14). But, today, I will make an exception. I thank you and your council for the service you gave in the past six years. You have strengthened the brothers in their faithfulness to the Gospel; you have shown respect for the old and the new, for the elderly and the young; you have sought to do faithfully the job you were given; you did not hide your mistakes; you have lovingly persevered in the face of unavoidable tensions. I rejoice to see how the brothers everywhere have been thankful for your service. Still, note well, John, that this is not yet perfect joy."

During the whole trip, John had listened more than spoken and had always remained patient. But at this point, he became somewhat impatient and said: "Brother Francis, I do not understand why you are saying all these things. What are you trying to tell me and my brothers at this Pentecost Chapter?"

Full of love and concern, Francis looked at Brother John and said to him: "When we come into the chapter hall at Santa Maria degli Angeli, we will receive some surprises, for which you will have to thank God. They will strengthen your faith in the values of the Gospel and will bring with them the meaning of true and perfect joy. If someone should complain against you at the Roman curia because of one-sided information and should ask there for protective letters and interventions against my express will; if someone should slander your option for the poor according to the Gospel as if it were Marxism; if someone should take local and specific mistakes and aberrations and exaggerate and generalize them; if someone should interpret a respectful and brotherly style as weakness; if someone should accuse you of divisions and manipulations, while at the same time they try to engineer manipulations and divisions from above; if someone should try to take away your freedom which I myself fought for at the Roman curia—this freedom which is a characteristic of our Order as a brotherhood; if someone should treat you as immature children and give you answers to questions you did not even ask, *then,* Brother John, you will all have perfect joy. It promises you many fruits of the Holy Spirit, whom you will all experience in a specially evident way, as will your Minister General. This joy graces all of you with a deepened faith in our Lord Jesus Christ, with a stronger unity than ever, and with love for many sisters and brothers, especially the poor. Therefore, if all of you keep your patience and hope in the face of everything that comes your way, then that will be true and perfect joy, a service to the Church and a promise of new and eternal life."

Then Brother John smiled, wrote down everything exactly, thanked Brother Francis, and, in the presence of many brothers, opened the Pentecost Chapter of 1985.

Santa Maria degli Angeli, Eve of Pentecost, 1985

2. How Brother Francis admonished his brothers through Brother Masseo that they should live not in the curias of nobles and prelates but in all simplicity among the people

Background: The dialogue between St. Francis and Brother Masseo, one of his first companions, is occasioned by the debates about the "Option for the Poor" at the 1985 General Chapter.

It happened one day that Brother Francis went with Brother Masseo from the little church called the Madonna del Riposo on the Roman road called the Aurelia towards the Vatican, in order to pray there at the tomb of the blessed Pope John XXIII. It chanced that he saw on his right, on a hill which the Romans call the Gelsomino, a church towering proudly into the Roman sky and ornamented with a great deal of marble and mosaic. It was dedicated to the Mother of God, Mediatrix of All Graces.

Brother Francis went into it with Brother Masseo because it pleased him to adore the Lord in all the churches of the whole world, irrespective of whether they were great or small. With great fervor he begged the Lord and his Mother, Mary, that the Gospel of the poor might be recognized more and more as the salt of the earth and as the city set on a hill, especially among his own brothers. At the same time he thanked the Lord for all those brothers and sisters who in the joy of the Gospel lived among the simple in a simple way in small groups and so played a part in renewing and building up the Church of Jesus Christ.

But since the church on the hill was very sound and solid and in no way in need of repair, Brother Francis, after spending an hour in fervent prayer, turned to go. Then Brother Masseo, who was known sometimes to give way to babbling words and childlike curiosity, said to him: "Do you know that it is the brothers of your Order who have built this church together with a large friary of thick walls? From this place they guide and govern and animate the brothers throughout the whole world. They call this house their curia, following thereby the example of kings and nobles as well as Roman prelates rather than the example of our Lord and your own clear precepts. From this place they can actually look down with pride day and night on the Lord Pope, to whom they are supposed to be subject in obedience and at whose feet they are supposed to be, and on the prelates of his curia. What do you say to that, Brother Francis?"

Thereupon, Francis was filled with great pain. But he remained very silent. He moved to the edge of that hill called the Gelsomino so that he could see the basilica of St. Peter and the papal curia in all its glory; he looked upon the marble facade of the Church of Our Lady. Then he bent down and wrote in the sand, just as the Lord Jesus had done in a well-known part of his Gospel.

Brother Masseo became very restless and pressed Brother Francis for an answer, saying: "How are your brothers today to recognize your will? Where do you want them to go and how do you want them to live?" After Brother Francis had continued for a while writing in the sand in silence, he decided to put Brother Masseo's obedience to the test in order to discover more clearly the Lord's will. He ordered him to turn round and round like a top, such as children love to play with, and not to stop. Every time that Brother Masseo fell down on the ground out of sheer dizziness and utter perplexity, Brother Francis told him to get up and begin again. Then, as he was spinning round in full swing, Francis suddenly told him to stop and asked him:

"Brother Masseo, in what direction are you facing?" Masseo, through whose simplicity there sometimes spoke the wisdom of

God, answered: "Towards St. Peter's, where at the Second Vatican Council there was talk of the Church of the Poor. Beyond that to the Portiuncula where you yourself lived with your brothers in simple huts and where today your brothers are gathered in the Pentecost Chapter, listening to the voice both of the Lord Pope and of the poor to discover anew their mission. Beyond that I am facing in the direction of Medellín, Puebla, Bahia, and all the lands in Occident and Orient where the brothers are living in the simplicity and joy of the Gospel among the poor, the Saracens, and those of other faiths." When he had finished speaking these words, he was so dizzy that he fell headlong down the hill and lay unconscious at the feet of the papal curia.

But Brother Francis thanked the Lord who is praised out of the mouths of the simple, cast a final glance at the towering walls behind him, hurried down the hill which his brothers had taken into their possession, picked up Brother Masseo, and went with him in the direction which the Lord wanted to show them, going before his brothers throughout the world.

St. Mary of the Angels, June 6, 1985

3. How Brother Francis reflected about old and new centers of learning, and how, illumined by the Holy Spirit, he gave some enlightened directives on this topic

Background: Another of the topics of the 1985 Chapter concerned the Order's Centers of Study: their renewal, their inculturation into the very different contexts of a worldwide Order. At the center of the debate stood the Order's University "Antonianum" in Rome.

One day Blessed Francis was at prayer in the chapel of Santa Maria degli Angeli. There he heard how the brothers outside in the fields and meadows were gathering for a Chapter of Mats to reflect on their life with God and certain other priorities, and to establish a plan of action, as they liked to call it, for the future. A certain Brother Luke, minister in England and Scotland, came to report on the glorious tradition of the brothers regarding studies in Oxford, Cambridge, and Canterbury. He praised the great masters of theology and philosophy and their wide-ranging works. He pointed out especially a certain Brother John of Duns in Scotland, who had no equal in subtleness. When he had said this, he was immediately followed by Brother Ives of Paris and Brother

Sartorius of Cologne. The first of them praised the former studies of the brothers in Gaul, which reached their most outstanding example in the seraphic teachings of Blessed Bonaventure and in the aforesaid John of Scotland. The other could testify, with the applause of many brothers, that this same John of Scotland had also been in Germany toward the end of his life and that he now lay buried in Cologne. Besides, he hoped that John would soon be declared blessed by the Pope on account of his zealous efforts.

All these conversations echoed in the chapel where Brother Francis was praying. And even though he himself wanted to remain simple and foolish, he thanked the Lord for the learning of so many outstanding and holy brothers of the past. As he went on listening to the brothers naming countless names and commentaries on the *Sentences* of Peter Lombard, with more interest in the past than in the coming Reign of God, Francis with simplicity of heart opened the Gospel. There he found the words that the letter kills and the Spirit gives life; he also found the other words of the Apostle Paul, according to which the former things have passed and new things have come to be.

He meditated long on these words in prayer before the Lord. Then another group of brothers arrived, among them a certain Brother Berard from Bologna, a Brother Anthony from Lisbon, and a Brother Angelus, a Carthaginian from Iberia. These also competed in holy zeal as to where the best traditions of learning and the most learned brothers and books richest in content were to be found: whether in Portugal or in Spain or in Italy. Though Francis had chosen as his own task itinerant apostolic preaching together with poverty and for that reason had once wanted to tear down a house of studies of the brothers in a certain town in Italy, still he was glad about all he now heard resounding in the chapel: how the brothers had done so much good through their theological learning. As the conversation went on and on, Francis recalled his own earlier admonition to the brothers that they not recall the deeds of the blesseds and the saints for the purpose of building up their own reputation. Then as he opened Holy Scriptures once more, he found by divine guidance the words about the sending of the disciples into the whole world and about evangelization and mission on all the continents.

On these words he meditated long in prayer before the Lord. After a while he heard how a certain Brother Alban from the northern half of the New World and a Brother Basil from the southern half of the New World hurried by. With great joy they brought news of new ways to investigate the secrets of God and the world. They counted up the new universities and centers where the brothers, following sound traditions and also new inspirations of the Spirit, taught and did research so that the Gospel of liberation could be announced as far as the regions of the Pacific Ocean, the Andes, and the Amazon. Then when one of the brothers of the Old World was asking about the meaning of the word *inculturation*, a certain Brother Irineu, a theologian, stood up and patiently explained that this word means that the Gospel has to be placed in the ground everywhere as a grain of seed so that the soil, which is at once the same everywhere and yet different, can produce fruits which will be the same everywhere and yet quite different.

Brother Francis rejoiced over what he heard and was very edified. Again he opened the Holy Bible and with God's help found words that one can know a tree by its fruits. These words too he pondered a long time before the Lord.

Suddenly a certain Brother Benvenute from a remote island kingdom in the Orient raised his voice. He said openly he had no money to build universities or to send students to study in the Old World. But he had erected an institute where the brothers and sisters of all the families of Brother Francis, answering the need for ongoing conversion to the Lord and for continuing formation, could study the writings of the Bible and the ideas and ideals of Blessed Brother Francis, enabling them to live the Gospel better and to announce it more effectively in word and deed. And since other brothers reported similar things, all were very edified. In all this they could all discern that the Lord at all times does great things and creates new things.

All these words reached the tiny chapel where Brother Francis was praying. After some time he opened the Bible once again to find with divine help the place where it says that one should not patch old garments with new cloth and that new wine does not belong in old skins. He then thanked the Lord also for these words and meditated on them a long time.

Suddenly on the road from Foligno to Santa Maria degli Angeli, there rose a great shout. It came from a group of brothers returning from Rome, where they live and work in a large and venerable house near the Lateran basilica. The group was brought by a certain Brother Maurilius, who had guarded the Holy Sepulcher in Jerusalem for many years, and by a certain Brother Thomas from Iberia, who was in charge of the *studium generale* in that house, which bore the name of Blessed Brother Anthony.

They joined the group of the other brothers and recounted how this large house in Rome was carrying on all those glorious traditions of the aforementioned places and universities. In the last hundred years, many brothers had received their formation there. The Lord Pope had paid a visit to the house and had praised it in one of his many letters. On the other hand, the brothers complained that many brothers in the world, especially in the more distant regions, no longer knew much about this Roman house dedicated to Blessed Brother Anthony. And they did not support it with their material help. Sometimes to their own detriment they even despised it.

When some brothers, curious to know just what went on there, wanted to learn more about that great center, one of the brothers went so far as to call to mind that even those great houses of Paris and Bologna were no longer in existence. At that moment the sky became dark and such a big storm arose that the brothers could not continue their conversation for quite some time. Then during a lull in the storm, Brother Thomas was answering questions. He pointed out that he had counted the students of the Order of Friars Minor one by one and had come to a very small total. On the other hand, he said, the number of universities in Rome had increased. At this point, a terrific bolt of lightning struck a nearby oak and the rain began to pour down, sending the brothers running in fright into the nearby woods, huts, and chapels to recommend their plight to God.

Brother Francis, however, who had been praying for a long time in the little chapel of Our Lady of the Angels and had heard everything, opened the Holy Scriptures once more and, wonderfully guided, found the words of the Lord according to which people indeed sometimes understand how to interpret the signs in the heavens and on the earth, in the clouds and the rain, but they cannot read the signs of the times. Even these words he pondered long in prayer before the Lord.

When the storm had passed an hour later and the sun shone again, the brothers came together anew to continue their deliberations. At that point, Brother Francis interrupted his prayer for a moment, left the chapel, came before the brothers from all round the world, and spoke in that succinct way which was uniquely his:

"Praised be you, my Lord, for all the past, the present and future study centers of the brothers, in which your secrets are truthfully investigated and put forth. But you, brothers, heed my voice: Think more about the future than about the past.

"Keep nothing back for yourselves and never consider anything your own, be it a stable place, a house, or rights and privileges. Be attentive to the anxieties and hopes, the questions and preoccupations of your brothers and sisters in the whole world. According to St. Paul's word, forget what lies behind and strain forward to what lies ahead (Phil 3:13). Read and meditate the signs also of the present times. But in all things observe charity."

With that, he went back into the chapel to pray. The brethren on their part were very edified by what they had heard and seen. Then they made their decisions.

Santa Maria degli Angeli, June 13, 1985

4. How some brothers and sisters meeting in Africa received a lesson on the subject of "inculturation and Franciscan formation"

Background: In November 1985 a number of those responsible for education in the Order from throughout the world met in Nairobi, Kenya, for an important conference which takes place every two years. The immediate occasion for this text was a nocturnal robbery of one of the Roman participants. The term "Transalpinus" refers to Europe north of the Alps.

In the year of the Lord 1985, while the brothers of St. Francis were meeting in the Pentecost Chapter, the Lord Pope John Paul II urged them to remain constant in faith, in unity, and in fidelity to their original charism. This he did by means of a letter, of a paternal discourse, and of the powerful help of some Roman prelates. Having done so, the Lord Pope himself set out on another of his numerous apostolic pilgrimages, this time to East Africa to celebrate there the Eucharist before immense crowds and to urge them to live the Christian life.

Then it was that many brothers and sisters of St. Francis decided to follow the same journey as the Lord Pope, conscious of their special obedience to the Holy See and to their own missionary charism. Thus they hoped to meditate in a very humble way and as the Lord might enlighten them about the encounter of the Gospel of our Lord Jesus Christ with the cultures of Africa, Asia, Oceania, America, and Europe. This they called "inculturation."

They prayed without ceasing to the Lord that he might show them also which teaching they should draw from this encounter to help towards their own conversion, a process which already for some time they had begun to call by the sophisticated name of ongoing formation. They also hoped that they might thus better introduce their young brothers to the Gospel, a process they called initial formation.

The city to which they directed their steps was called Nairobi. The brothers and sisters had as a leader a certain Brother Hermannus Transalpinus, who for some time now had been based in Rome. Following one of the many and blessed traditions of the Order of Friars Minor, they lodged with the sons of St. Benedict, who received them with open arms in a house which bore the name *Amani*. In that distant land the word means peace, that which the Lord promised to people of goodwill and is so loved by the sons and daughters of St. Francis. They were all immensely happy when they came to this house and learned the meaning of the word *Amani*.

The lesser brothers and the sisters who had gathered there from around the world were most anxious to follow, also in Africa, the example of their father and brother, Francis. That is why they wished to understand the word inculturation and all that it might mean, more by living experience than by hearing learned conferences, by listening rather than by speaking, by obedience to every creature rather than by teaching and wordy preaching. That indeed is what the Lord had asked and that is what Francis had left them in his writings.

They wished to understand that whatever the circumstances, the Gospel of our Lord Jesus Christ must be implanted in every country under the sun to produce everywhere fruit which is the same yet different. They wished further to understand that the Church and the fraternity of the Lesser Brothers, which for a long time had been very Roman, should be understood "in a more catholic way" since the Gospel and the true brotherhood of all people with the same Father in heaven knows no frontiers of language or culture. Also they very much wished to learn from the poor, as the Lord in the first place had asked them to do and as the Chapter of Pentecost just recently had asked them to do through its "Plan of Action." In a word, they sought more and more the formation that comes through lived experience, a process they called "induction" rather than the formation that comes from theorizing, a process called "deduction," and that because in a truly marvelous way the Lord himself "induced" their father and brother, Francis, to live among the poor.

The brothers and sisters conversed for several days and became more and more sensitive to the voice of the poor; they discovered a great faith in churches, chapels, and basic ecclesial communities in those regions. For long periods they prayed together in diverse tongues. They even made a fraternal visit to a great and colorful variety of wild animals in a well-known national park, following another blessed tradition of the sisters and Lesser Brothers, to bring the wish of peace even to the animals. Whereupon the brothers were most edified and indeed exhausted by all that they had heard and seen. At Compline, after begging the Lord for a "quiet night" and "a perfect end," they retired for a well-earned rest.

But lo, on that same night, thanks to the wise providence of the Lord, all the brothers, particularly those from Rome, received an unscheduled and most interesting lesson on inculturation and Franciscan formation. Three robbers armed with rocks and long knives forced their way into that house called Amani—to be precise, into the cell of a certain Brother Saul. He is the one who, together with a certain Brother Augustinus Venetus, works in the Roman headquarters of the Lesser Brothers, formulating important plans for the formation of the brothers and for the renewal of the Roman study center dedicated to St. Anthony. In order to complete their shameful undertaking, the robbers commanded Brother Saul to observe complete silence while they began stealing all the documents, all the plans, and other things. Then they left him locked in his cell and disappeared into the darkness of the African night.

Brother Saul, who during this unscheduled visit kept praying for all he was worth to the Lord, mindful of the words of the Apostle Paul who says that the strength of the Lord's disciple is to be found in his own weakness, then began to call for help, roaring and screaming to be freed from his enforced captivity. With so much yelling and banging on the door, Brother Hermannus Transalpinus was at last awakened. He was sleeping in the next cell and in some miraculous way was spared a visit from the robbers. Thus was Brother Saul set free and all gathered round to console him.

When night had passed and the dawn came, all the brothers made their way to the little chapel of the sons of St. Benedict to pray and give thanks to the Lord for all that he permits, even that which is bitter, so that God may change it into sweetness of soul and body, just as Francis himself experienced.

When all had been absorbed for a long time in contemplation, in obedience to the first priority of the last general chapter, they heard, each in his own tongue, as is the case in genuine inculturation, the voice of St. Francis which said: "My sons and daughters, hear my voice and open your hearts to all that the Lord wishes to say to you. Allow yourselves to receive formation from every source: from our Lord Jesus Christ, from his Gospel which you have promised to live, from the poor of every land, even from robbers and brigands from whom you have received such a formative visit. Pray for all who persecute you and wish to do you harm. These are the Lord's instruments when he wishes you to receive formation and inculturation according to the Gospel. For everything which happens to you in this life, as you yourselves have written in so many documents of your brotherhood, helps towards your conversion, towards the formation of all the brothers, and towards the evangelization of the poor. Even if you had to suffer much more, even if you should lose your lives in the formation of your brothers, even if your headquarters in Rome should be set on fire and all your documents, plans of action and priorities should become the prey of Brother Fire or be stolen by thieves, you should ever and always give thanks to the Lord for the lessons on formation and inculturation given to you through God's goodness. Indeed, these lessons result from lived experience and deepen the experience of living, as you yourselves have always desired. For truly it is in weakness and in the contemplation of the reality of the world that surrounds you that you will find the strength to be inculturated more in accordance with the Gospel, a t all times and in all places. Render thanks to the Lord for everything and give thanks as well for our brother robbers. Amani."

On hearing these words all were extremely edified and consoled. With renewed enthusiasm they concluded their meeting. Some traveled to fraternities in neighboring countries to visit the brothers. Afterwards they returned, each to his own country. The rest returned to Rome to translate into concrete action all that they had heard and experienced.

Nairobi, November 9, 1985

1986

5. How certain brothers from Rome reflected on the Admonition of Brother Francis which says, "Where there is peace and contemplation, there is neither care nor restlessness" (Adm 27)

Background: In the autumn of 1986 the Order's leadership under John Vaughn held a meeting in Vittorio Veneto and spent several days of retreat on the island of San Francesco del Deserto in the lagoon of Venice.

It was the beautiful month of September in the year of our Lord 1986. The leaders of the peoples had declared an International Year of Peace. Shortly after the feast of the Stigmata of our Father and Brother Francis, the Minister of the whole brotherhood with his councillors, also called definitors, made his way towards the north of the Italian peninsula to a city called Vittorio Veneto in the province of Treviso to a humble convent under the obedience of the minister of that region, Augustinus Venetus.

At the beginning of the second year of his second six-year term of ministry, John of Santa Barbara, the Minister of all the brothers, joined by those brothers called councillors and relying on the powerful help of the prayers of many brothers throughout the world, desired to study the numerous, diverse, and difficult tasks which lay ahead. Together they wished to help in putting into practice the Order's Six-Year Plan, which had been entrusted to them by the last general chapter, held at the Portiuncula. This plan should promote the three priorities—thus the brothers prefer to call them—of this present time: the contemplative dimension, preferential option for the poor, especially in relation to justice and peace, and formation to a missionary spirit.

During their short periods of recreation in that friary, the brothers devoted themselves to prayer and song, to fraternal dialogue with the hospitable brothers and sisters of that region and fraternity, to harvesting the grapes in the garden, and to imparting Franciscan formation to three young cats which wandered about the cloisters of that venerable friary. They also made an excursion to the province's high mountains—called the Dolomites—where they were afforded a special opportunity of singing the praises of Sister Rain and Sister Fog.

Once those fruitful days were over, the brothers decided to pass two more days in Venice for the purpose of living the contemplative dimension themselves, instead of talking about it first and then recommending it to others. In order to do this—and in obedience to the brothers and sisters of Venice, particularly to Minister Augustinus—they agreed to retire to a hermitage on an island in the Venetian lagoon, the island called "St. Francis of the Desert." This is the island where St. Francis paused on returning from his apostolic journey of peace to the East. Here he hoped to find peace himself and to seek God in prayer (LM 9). And even though it was most difficult, if not impossible, for the brothers from Rome to observe a fast—a feature also present in Vittorio Veneto—because of the watchful motherly attentions of the brothers and sisters who had welcomed them, they tried at any rate to seek conversion of heart and to pray for world peace, in accordance with the admonition of their Father and Brother Francis, already quoted.

And so the Minister General and his companions, guided personally by the minister from Venice, set out in a gondola. This boat very nearly capsized due to the volume of the documents and memoranda from their Roman curia taken on board. They passed beneath the Bridge of Sighs, meditating with deep intensity on their problems and anxieties, and came in front of that church where Marco Polo is buried. In silence they admired his courage as a discoverer. Then they came to that island called "The Desert," where the Lesser Brothers live. Since St. Francis rested there, it is held in great veneration even to this day. At the pier they received a cordial welcome from all the friars, who showed them to their humble cells, then led them to the chapel and finally to the refectory all laid out for a hearty feast.

For the space of several hours the brothers in quiet meditation dedicated themselves to the contemplation of the reality of God, endeavoring to drive far away all care and restlessness. With the first light of dawn they became aware that, as St. Bonaventure had described, this island in the middle of the Venetian lagoon was inhabited not only by friars but also by enormous flocks of birds of different kinds, and by one cow and one dog. And as the same Seraphic Doctor had already described, the birds, alighting on the branches, "set up an animated warbling"(LM 9). Since the brothers from Rome, however, did not enjoy the power of prophetic language like Francis—who had caused the birds to observe silence so that he might peacefully recite the Divine Office and then gave them permission to continue their warbling, the brothers simply had to sing the divine praises accompanied by the birds.

During the whole of the first day in the "Desert," the brothers meditated on the words of St. Paul in the hope of shedding light on their own lives: "Who shall separate us from the love of Christ? Will hardship, or distress, or persecution, or famine, or nakedness, or peril, or the sword?"(Rom 8:35).

For the meditations of the second day, however, a brother living among the transalpine fogs chose an episode taken from Thomas of Celano's *Second Life of Francis* (2Cel 64), offering an explanation of it so that the others might apply it to their own lives. The story told how Brother Francis was on a journey towards a leprosarium, carried on a donkey. He passed through the town of Borgo San Sepolcro, almost crushed by the multitude of onlookers, but was so absorbed in "contemplation of the divine mysteries" that he was oblivious to what was happening around him. So when they had already passed through Borgo San Sepolcro, he asked his companions what time they might arrive at that lively place.

In silent prayer and fervent dialogue among themselves, with nature and with the animals of that island, the brothers asked themselves in line with the second priority whether they also were on a journey towards a leprosarium and towards the poor; furthermore, whether they tried to dedicate themselves also to contemplation while on their journeys, whether they were content with the back of a donkey on these same journeys, and finally, whether they were capable of devoting themselves to contemplation from the back of a donkey. At any rate they asked insistently of the Lord to grant them the gift of quiet, tranquillity, and sweetness in contemplation, not only in their chapels and on solitary islands but also when they were hurrying through continents or when they stopped over in big cities of this world; likewise, when they found themselves surrounded by people or in the midst of their own brothers.

With great humility the brothers from Rome had to admit that in this respect they found themselves far behind Brother Francis. However, through meditation on the word of God and the Gospel example of their Seraphic Father, they felt so consoled and strengthened that they adopted various good resolutions, giving thanks to the Lord for all things.

At the end of their stay on the island of "St. Francis of the Desert," the brothers were treated to a special rendering of music and song precisely by that brother who formerly had been the minister of the Province of Venice and was now the guardian of the island. His name is Florindus.

Fortified in spirit and in body and accompanied by the polyphonic choir of his councillors, Brother John of Santa Barbara celebrated a closing Mass in which more brothers from Venice took part, having arrived hurriedly in boats and gondolas. To all he addressed words of fatherly exhortation and brotherly gratitude.

Finally the brothers from Rome returned to the mainland and each one separately went out to meet the brothers of the whole world, exhorting them to live according to the Gospel and the three evangelical priorities already mentioned, beginning with contemplation. They carried with them a letter from the Minister General inviting all to fast and pray on 27 October, the Day of Prayer for Peace in Assisi, in union with the Lord Pope and the heads of world religions. In their hearts, however, they carried the message of the "Desert," namely, peace with oneself and the hope of a new life. They felt purified and fortified in the desert, through prayer and the encounter with God, to dedicate themselves to greater and deeper contemplation. In fact, they were prepared to fight for the justice of the Kingdom of God—should the Lord call on them—and for the ongoing renewal of the brotherhood according to the Gospel.

St. Francis of the Desert, October 3, 1986

Chapter 2
1987-1988

1987

6. How some brothers from East and West discovered the meaning of the psalmist's words, "And by my God, I can leap over a wall" (Ps 18:29)

Background: From 1970 until 1990 the Order held what were called East-West Encounters for the members living in the former "Socialistic States." These meetings always took place around the feast of the Epiphany (January 6) in a diocesan house on the Pappelallee in East Berlin. They constituted for many years an important link with the Franciscans in East Germany, Poland, Hungary, and Czechoslovakia. Friars from Western countries and from Rome were always there.

Shortly before the feast of the Epiphany of the Lord in the year 1987, as Transalpine Europe was in the grip of winter darkness and frost which indeed did not spare Cisalpine Europe, behold brothers came from the rising of the sun and from its setting to Berlin in the Brandenburg region in order to worship the Lord who is the light in the darkness and to greet one another, confirming each other in living the Gospel. Some of them came from those fraternities which are in Scandinavia, Saxony, Lower Germany, Thuringia, the Rhineland, Austria, both Americas, Africa, and also Rome in Latium. They gathered in the western part of Berlin and celebrated there a liturgy of thanksgiving for their happy arrival. Brother Anglicus from Rome delivered greetings from the Minister General and Brother Transalpinus spoke briefly, as Brother Francis had recommended, about the three wise men as examples of a preferential option for the poor, which he said would always be the evangelical fruit of an exclusive option for Jesus. Meanwhile, in the eastern part of the same city, brothers were assembling from those fraternities which are to be found in the East, namely in Pannonia, Bohemia, Moravia, Slovakia, and Carpathia. Yes, they even came from the motherland of our Lord Pope gloriously reigning in Rome. As a lodging they had chosen a house dedicated to St.

Joseph, where for their part they gave thanks for their happy arrival, contemplated the Incarnation of our Lord as light and comfort in a divided and peaceless world, and awaited the arrival of their brothers from the other part of the city in order to "treat fruitfully of these things which appertain to God" (RegNB 18:1) together with them.

And indeed it happened that the last-named brothers set out in the early morning of the following day in the most bitter cold to reach the house of St. Joseph on the other side of the great wall which divides that city. For they knew that other brothers were waiting for them there in order to worship the Lord together with them and to offer him and each other their gifts—the gold of true brotherhood under one Lord, the frankincense of a peaceful and peace-giving spirit, and the myrrh of mutual encouragement to serve the Lord more generously wherever each one might find himself. Now as the brothers from the West were being questioned by the men guarding that great wall about their purpose and the place they came from, the brothers replied fearlessly and in accordance with the truth, "We are Friars Minor, brothers of penance from Assisi, subject to all people. We carry no arms and only very little money. It is our desire to worship the Lord in the churches and chapels of your city and to greet members of our family in St. Joseph's house." The guards were astonished at these words and asked themselves what they might mean. Since they did not often come across people with such intentions, they decided to test the purity of the brothers' motives. And so some of the brothers were invited to bring out and show everything they were carrying in their poverty-stricken pockets, bags, sleeves, capuches, and knapsacks.

In this way there appeared only a few insignificant coins plus the psalters and breviaries which they always carried with them for the praise of God. Some of them did not even have these because they had resolved that on this day they would, in accordance with the mind and directions of Brother Francis, pray the Our Father (RegB 3). A certain brother from the Netherlands, however, coordinator in his conference for questions of justice and peace, drew from the depths of his knapsack an innocent flute and displayed it. The guards thereupon called on him to play it. Then the brother played most melodiously—though for his uninformed listeners in a manner most unfamiliar—the last verse of the *Canticle of the Creatures* of Brother Francis. And once more the conviction which the brother from the Netherlands cherished was demonstrated to be true, namely that music represents a universal value and has a pacifying effect on all men and women of goodwill, for the guards listened and appeared almost ready to smile.

Since the peaceful intentions of the brothers were by now perfectly obvious, the guards allowed them to pass beyond the wall to the other part of the city. So the brothers parted from them with the words, "The Lord give you peace."

When all the brothers had finally gathered together in one place, they rejoiced greatly, gave one another the kiss of peace, and recounted the difficulties of their long journeys. They also counted one another and so realized that no fewer than seventy brothers had followed the star which had come to rest over St. Joseph's house. They gave thanks to the Lord, spread out the above-mentioned gifts and sang in thanksgiving Psalm 18. As they came to the verse which says, "By my God, I can leap over the wall," they gave renewed thanks for the special grace of a worldwide brotherhood which knows no frontiers and is divided by no walls.

Throughout the first day the brothers who had hurried here from all the aforementioned parts of the world recounted to one another the signs and wonders which the Lord had worked among them in recent times but also the manifold experiences of perfect joy which all of them had gone through not only in the East, but also in the West, and even in the South, that is, in Rome. They all confirmed each other with truly brotherly conversation in their determination to live better the liberating Gospel of our Lord within all the lands, systems, and ideologies and to implant the seeds of peace and justice everywhere, but above all in their own hearts. They resolved to do this through true observance of their first priority, which is grateful contemplation of the epiphany of our Lord in all creation, in all religions, in human history, on the faces of their brothers and sisters, especially the poor and little ones. They all appreciated in a deeper way that they belonged to a true brotherhood. For this they praised God in ever new psalms and songs as well as in many tongues and languages.

On the evening of this first day, a certain young friar named Augustine, who had come from a far country under the Southern Cross, celebrated the Eucharist with them. He spoke during it about the hope of the poor and of the "liberating praxis"—as it had been rightly called in these years—of the basic ecclesial communities. These, as the brother pointed out, were arising not out of earthly knowledge but rather from Christian's contemplating their lives in the light of the Holy Scriptures. All those who heard about the humble service of so many brothers in these communities were greatly edified. Late into the night the tales told by the brothers continued. The brothers also sang some songs which were not to be found in their hymnbooks and psalters. But in the end—it was almost midnight—the brothers from the West returned through the great wall to the other side for their nightly repose. For so the guards had told them to do.

After a short but well-deserved night's rest, the brothers made their way the following morning to the East in order to continue the spiritual exchanges with their brothers. Once more they called down peace upon the guards at the wall and once more they were allowed to pass, this time without having to prove the innocence of their intent. On the other side they were already being awaited with great longing. Once more they began the day with a meditation on Holy Scripture. This time they spoke about Jericho (Jos 6) and how according to the Letter to the Hebrews (11:30) it was faith which caused the walls of that city to fall down. They insistently begged the Lord to bestow on them in the churches and chapels, but also in their encounters with one another and with all men and women of goodwill, a strong faith to break down all the walls which stand in the way of the spread of God's Kingdom and peace, not least the walls of fear, prejudice, and blindness in their own hearts.

After that a certain Brother Carolus from the northern part of the New World, who was known to be a pious and wise man and who had collaborated in drawing up the new General Constitutions, spoke up and instructed all those present about the spirit and the letter of the new laws which the last Pentecost Chapter had approved under the presidency of a prelate of the Holy Roman Church. Brother Carolus demonstrated that it was the meaning of these laws to guide the brothers in their life according to the Gospel, in accordance with the Church's mission, basing themselves upon sound traditions and being aware of the signs of the present times. Above all he drew attention to the fact that in a world of walls, class divisions, and injustice, where according to our Lord, "The kings of the Gentiles lord it over them; and those who in authority over them are called benefactors" (Lk 22:25), our brotherhood is called to be a sign of a new world where "it cannot be that way with you" (Lk 22:26, NAB). The Lesser Brothers should be, as Brother Francis wished and the general chapter rediscovered, equal among themselves. They should be without any privileges and be Gospel witnesses of brotherhood to all people, especially to the enslaved and those deprived of their liberty, but also to the great ones and the rulers. The more they heard about the new laws, the last general chapter, and its evangelical priorities, the more the brothers rejoiced at the new responsibility which arose from all this and the more insistently they prayed that the Roman curia might confirm their mission as a brotherhood "without gloss." For this confirmation was still lacking at that time, in spite of long and patient waiting and unceasing prayers and petitions. In the concluding celebration of the Eucharist, the brothers gave thanks for the gift of these two days. At the same time they prayed to the Lord to make them all a living sign of brotherhood in a divided world and society.

So the brothers from East, West, North, and South concluded their meeting and returned—sometimes by a different route from that by which they had come—to their homelands and fraternities; two of them went to their general curia in Rome, "to tell what is good and to do what is good and to praise the Lord" (RegNB 17:19).

Berlin, January 1987

7. On the manner in which some Lesser Brothers, gathered at Monte Casale, reflected on the priority of "Justice and Peace"

Background: The General Chapter of 1985 had laid down three guidelines ("priorities") for the Order: contemplation, justice and peace through an option for the poor, and mission. The following text takes as its theme the Franciscan commitment to peace, justice, and the safeguarding of creation. The fictitious place of the action is a meeting of the Order's International Council for Justice and Peace.

During those days—more precisely during the six years stretching from 1985 to 1991—there arose within the brotherhood of the Franciscan Order a lengthy, animated, and many-sided but, at the same time, fraternal discussion on a priority of the Gospel life which their Father, Brother Francis, had left them. This priority had been given greater emphasis in the last Pentecost Chapter. It is one which Brother Francis taught consistently. It is a life without property; it is the preferential option for the poor; it is the commitment to justice and peace.

Several brothers throughout the world had already begun to practice this directive courageously and fearlessly and to live out its consequences, while others, with an equally holy zeal for the Kingdom of God and the good of the brotherhood, considered this priority together with some of the things it implied as dangerous, liberal, and modernist. To these it seemed entirely too "political" and "horizontal." The task of discerning the origins, the content, the purpose, and the implications of this priority in the light of the Gospel seemed a difficult one. Thus the Brother Minister General, in union with his general council, decided that there should be a meeting in the year 1987 of those brothers who in their conferences had been given the task of introducing, patiently explaining, and putting into practice the Franciscan commitment to justice and peace. By the grace of God such a meeting would bring all to a better knowledge of the second priority adopted by the general chapter in such a way that all the brothers, wherever the Lord might have sent them, could observe "in a more catholic way" (Test 34) the Rule of Francis and the Gospel of the Lord Jesus.

Many brothers had proposed to the Brother Minister that he should convoke such an important meeting in the Republic of the Philippine Islands in order to give all the participants, especially those coming from Rome, the unique possibility of seeing and studying how it was possible—especially through prayer and the peace-oriented action of the local bishops plus those of many brothers and sisters—for God to "bring down the powerful from their thrones and lift up the lowly" (Lk 1:52); in effect how a more just and democratic government should be established for the benefit of the poor.

Others among the brothers proposed that the meeting should be held in the American subcontinent so that they could see and behold with the eyes of the poor the conditions of life there, as they had an opportunity of doing during the famous meeting at Bahia in the year of the Lord 1983. All this group had for many years begun to be contemplative in liberation and liberating in contemplation. Many brothers and sisters in the faith were firmly convinced that through the liberating action on the part of these local churches many branches and new fruits had blossomed on the tree of the Church and likewise on that of the brotherhood—so much so that other local churches and fraternities who had not yet come to experience this praxis and contemplation were surprised and amazed.

Having heard all these proposals, the Brother Minister decided to hold a meeting of the delegates of the conferences plus the members of the general council at Monte Casale on the Italian peninsula in the very place where Brother Francis had taught his first companions the Gospel manner of living with the poor, the marginalized, and even with robbers and bandits in an attitude of Christian peace and evangelical justice.

Thus it happened that the above-mentioned brothers joined one another in the famous hermitage of Monte Casale to be mutually evangelized and to teach one another what a life of strict observance should be today in accordance with the second priority of the last general chapter.

Having assembled in Monte Casale and having contemplated and for a goodly period called upon God, who according to the teachings of Brother Francis is also named justice and moderation (LaudDei), they began to read in silence that well-known writing in which our Founder clearly teaches that the brothers should behave towards all in a fraternal manner and without prejudice, that the poor and thieves have a right to share our goods, and that it is through respect and justice that a solid base for lasting peace is built (LP 115; Fior 26). It may be well to recall that the brothers who lived in Monte Casale in Francis's day dedicated themselves exclusively to the contemplative dimension. However, they felt very perturbed and disturbed by some thieves who lived in a nearby forest and who from time to time approached the friary to beg for alms. Unfortunately, they had also stolen from some people who were passing through the forest on their way to bring food to the brothers of Francis. Being very angry with the thieves, these brothers upbraided them for their manner of living. They gave them a few dry crumbs of bread, adding pious and severe counsels about how they should change their detestable way of life.

The story goes on to say that on his arrival at Monte Casale Brother Francis proposed an alternative manner of action towards those poor thieves. He insisted that the brothers should always offer them the very best bread and the best wine that they had available with great confidence in the Lord, the giver of all good things. They should give them other delicacies also, all of them sweetened by sentiments of respect, of solidarity, and of justice. Francis explained that only by sharing, compassion, and a genuinely Christian humane attitude can thieves be brought to conversion. And so it happened that once the brothers had been won over to the practice of justice and peace, the thieves were touched

to the heart and opened themselves to the word of God and were
converted. Some of them even entered the brotherhood.

For a long period of time all the brothers allowed the message
conveyed by this story to penetrate their hearts. Then, moved by
holy zeal plus the reading of the Sacred Scriptures, they began to
interpret the narrative in the light of their own experiences,
helped by modern social science. By this means they hoped to gain
a clearer vision of their commitment in favor of justice and peace
according to the mind of Brother Francis.

First to speak was a certain Brother Peter from a region in
France where he had labored together with many other brothers of
St. Francis as a simple worker in a factory. He earned his
livelihood by the work of his own hands and in this way shared
the life of the labor force as well as the lot of the unemployed
when he was out of work. With evident emotion he told them how
throughout the whole of human history the working class had been
abused and marginalized by unjust and discriminatory treatment at
the hands of the powerful. The result was that, whether due to
indigence, lockout or unemployment, to low wages, or all that today
goes under the name of unjust structures, the poor had been reduced
to misery, to desperation, and, at times, to revolution. He urgently
requested all the brothers, wherever they might be, whether in
hermitages, in small fraternities, in parishes, or in large houses, to
throw open their hearts and their houses to the poor and the
marginalized. In this way might be fulfilled the mandate of the
meeting in Bahia which laid down that all the brothers should be
instruments of justice and peace. This should indeed involve much
prayer but it should also involve personal and concrete support of
trade unions and all other initiatives suitable for the promotion
and protection of the dignity and rights of people (*The Gospel
Challenges Us, 31*).

Another brother, a native of a country belonging to the Old
Continent, a man trained in the modern sciences but at the same
time very devoted to the things of God, had meditated upon and
then duly analyzed the occurrence at Monte Casale in this way.
Without mincing words he declared that the thieves mentioned in
the text were those who today are the victims of an exploiting
class. This brother went on to say that this statement did not imply
that he wished to be the defender or protagonist of a certain
atheistic social theory which sprang up in German lands at the end
of the last century and which had been rejected several times by
the Roman dicastery which defends the purity of the faith. The

brother went on to say that in order to overcome and finally eradicate such idolatrous and abominable ideologies, together with their lamentable consequences, it was essential to eliminate their causes and their starting point. There is a need to address the injustices within social groups and within nations by introducing that kind of fraternity and justice which are the visible and tangible signs of the Kingdom of God. He added that unless there is justice for all there will never be peace in this world. He ended his remarks by recalling that the Lord Pope, in his innumerable letters to the nations and his frequent pilgrimages to those places where the Lord appears miraculously in the poor, had never ceased to proclaim and to recall this doctrine: "Peace is a work of justice." All the brothers meditated on this important testimony for a long time.

Next, another European brother intervened to state his objection in a respectful but nevertheless very clear manner. He said the Lord Pope had forbidden by virtue of holy obedience all bishops, priests, brothers, and sisters from participating in the rough and tumble and the vices of human politics. He further recalled that all the brothers were obliged to proclaim and to live out the preferential option for the poor in the silence of their hearts and in penance rather than by wordy declarations or by showy demonstrations. Further, he emphasized that the same Lord Pope in his letter to the last general chapter had pointed out that poverty ought to be part of the life of the same Lesser Brothers before they began to proclaim it to others. Finally, he declared his conviction that people in general and the poor in particular need to be freed not so much from unjust structures as from their own sins.

At this point a brother from Africa intervened to enlighten the assembled brothers concerning his interpretation of the events of Monte Casale. His understanding was that Brother Francis, through supernatural love, his own conversion, and his mystical as well as practical love for the poor and marginalized, had created a new reality, one which, implied "political" consequences. Or was it not, rather, a healthy and very necessary form of social politics which Brother Francis had elaborated by means of love, namely, the freeing of the thieves from their poverty, marginalization, and isolation in the forest, bringing them back again to society and in this way contributing to a more just and consequently a more peaceful society? This brother maintained the thesis, a daring but brilliant one, that the commitment to justice and peace is an expression of faith in God who creates, transforms, and perfects creation, a creation always rooted in divine mystery but one which always carries with it concrete attitudes of liberation, even with respect to what may be justly called "social sin."

Those who had heard the two foregoing interpretations did not wish to contradict the one or the other position since each one seemed to justify itself.

Then the brother who came from Central America wished to round off these points of view. He said he was convinced that he could apply the Franciscan lesson of Monte Casale to entire communities of his vast subcontinent. Before undertaking his journey he had passed by the city which bears the name of Our Most Holy Redeemer, San Salvador, in order to pray at the tomb of that archbishop who had been cowardly assassinated by powerful enemies of the poor while he celebrated the Holy Eucharist. He related how the simple people of those regions had already canonized Bishop Oscar Romero and had proclaimed him a martyr and protector of the poor. The poor now held his tomb in veneration as also the tombs of some Lesser Brothers who had been assassinated for the cause of the faith and their public stand in defense of those who suffer. Before the tomb of the blessed Romero there were more people to be found in fervent prayer to the Lord of Life than were to be seen in many churches and sacred places in the city of Rome.

The brother went on to say that in modern times entire nations have become the innocent victims of the greed and warlike intentions of a few powerful individuals. Was it not true, he exclaimed, that at the meetings of Medellín and Puebla the bishops had solemnly proclaimed that "the rich are becoming every day richer and the poor every day poorer?" Is it not remarkable that the Lord Pope had confirmed such a statement? The brother ended in tears, maintaining that it was necessary to speak of "social sin" and to evangelize not only people individually but sinful and unjust structures as well. Only when the rich, under the influence of such an integral evangelization, relinquish their privileges, their arms, and their protective barriers and share the goods of the earth with others, restoring to everyone their dignity and their rights, only then shall there be true peace. "That is my reading of Monte Casale today."

There followed a period of humble prayer and of respectful meditation on what had been said. Then another brother from Europe expressed the desire to speak. He is the one who represents those regions and countries which lie to the east. He began by thanking everybody for the solidarity and help which the brothers of other parts of the world had given to these provinces in difficult moments, particularly in moments of persecution and poverty. Nevertheless he was forced to reproach fraternally some brothers from regions which lie towards the west for their imprudent and premature dialogue with dominant ideologies not only in eastern countries but also with virulent ones in other parts of the world. It is impossible, he held, to trust in the proclamations of peace made by the powerful in the socialist countries because they do not recognize God nor do they grant any freedom to the Church.

These distinctions were not underestimated by the brothers since they corresponded to the truth. However, a brother from the Far East wished to submit to their judgment his vision of what should be the authentic manner of dialogue. In this context the brother recalled not only the gesture of Francis with the aforementioned thieves, but also the eloquent gesture of the Lord Pope in Assisi on October 27 of last year when, humbly confessing his faith in Jesus Christ, he had offered to Saracens and people of different faiths his friendship and Christian hospitality, opening up to all without distinction a dialogue free of prejudices, as well as praying with them for peace in the world. Was not this, asked the brother, a truly prophetic gesture? Is it not also our duty to see in all people of goodwill, in all races, religions, and convictions the good and positive worth which God, the Lord of all, wishes to encourage in all women and men at all times—not only in Christians, who many times in history have not known how to fulfill the commandments of the Lord?

And so the brother from Asia expressed his amazement at the fact that according to some news reports published in the bulletin *Fraternitas* of the general curia, several European brothers had recently declared their intention of electing as patron of justice and peace John of Capistrano, a holy, but unfortunately warlike, man. For it was a matter of common knowledge that this famous brother, in accordance with the spirit of the time, had distinguished himself more by the fact that he had organized punitive missions and crusades against the Muslims, the Turks, the Jews, the Utraquists, and the Hussites than by the sweetness and spirit of meekness and peacemaking of his Father Francis. The Asian brother underlined the fact that by a document of the curia of the Lord Pope, John of Capistrano had already been proclaimed patron of military chaplains. No better patron of the second priority and of active nonviolence was to be found than Brother Francis himself, for the glory of God and the good of all humanity.

Finally a brother from the northern portion of the Americas decided to give his contribution. He said, first of all, that it was a deep conviction of his and of several other brothers from those territories that from contemplation of the Word made flesh and conversion of the heart to the Lord of life there would and should emerge visible and unmistakable gestures against death and in favor of life and peace. And he pointed out one example. Many brothers and sisters of those regions had the custom of coming together in prayer and severe fasting at those places where the powerful were constructing and testing very powerful arms destined for intercontinental wars, even for interplanetary wars. These arms, he said, are an insult to God and are the cause of death to many poor people even here and now. For even before they are set off, the money spent on their production should be considered as stolen from the poor, many of whom are dying of hunger and illness. Public expressions of protest such as those taking place in the Nevada desert, for example, should not be considered in any way "political." Rather they are a public act of faith in God and at the same time a faithful following of Brother Francis, who, in his *Letter to the Rulers of the Peoples*, had made an appeal to the sovereignty of God and to the value of all created things, particularly of human life. With the same mentality with which Francis had offered bread, wine, and cheese freely and generously to the brother thieves, so also ought we, Lesser Brothers of today, contribute to the construction of a new society and of a new global sociopolitical order. This was definitely his reading of the episode of Monte Casale: The poor then and now are not thieves but rather the victims of cultural and economic dependence. They have a right not so much to alms as to the goods of others and to our love. Brothers, said he, let us begin!

Once again all remained in silence and in prayer. They gave thanks to the Lord for having shown them the holy mandate which he had given them, namely, to follow Jesus poor and crucified in affective and effective solidarity with the poor of all times. And since the commitment to the second priority of the six-year period had by everyone's help been clarified in such a wonderful way, they thought it inopportune to approve new laws and directives. For they said that they had already been given sufficient norms in recent general chapters and plenary councils. Rather they simply and unanimously enjoined on Brother Gerard, the Order's coordinator of all justice and peace matters, that he should continue his work in the spirit of Monte Casale and be assured of the support of many brothers in the provinces and vice-provinces.

With that the brothers closed this fruitful meeting with a prayer which the Lord had inspired them to say at that moment in honor of the Marian year recently proclaimed and for their whole mission:

> Hail Mary, full of the hope of the poor of all the world. The Lord is with you. Blessed are you among the oppressed, and blessed is the fruit of your womb, liberation through Jesus.

> Holy Mary, Mother of God and of the poor, pray for us, sinners and faint-hearted, so that we may trust in the Spirit of the Lord now while peoples are suffering and striving for justice, and also at the hour when they shall attain justice so that all of us may live in peace. Amen.

And the brothers returned to their respective fraternities to put into practice all that they had heard and seen.

Monte Casale, Lent 1987

8. On the manner in which some brothers from Rome discovered the importance of music and other arts for the work of evangelization

Background: In the autumn of 1987 the general leadership of the Order met together in the hermitage of St. Antony in Monte Paolo (Forlì). The following text has used musical and culinary ideas to reflect on the three priorities of the Order (#9).

In the year of the Lord 1987, at a time when many hundreds of bishops were holding a discussion in Rome on the role of many millions of lay people in the Church and when the curia of the Lord Pope had declared the brotherhood to be a "clerical Order," it happened that the council of the Order of Lesser Brothers, also called the general definitorium, came together for a long session under the guidance of Brother John. The place chosen on this occasion was a hermitage in Emilia Romagna called Monte Paolo, a place dedicated to the memory of Brother Anthony of Padua who often had set out from this place on a mission of itinerant preaching.

During their stay of almost ten days the brothers from Rome, mindful of the example of Brother Francis, solemnly promised obedience to a certain Brother Damian, just as Francis had submitted himself in obedience to Brother Masseo (Fior, 3rd Consideration) on Mount La Verna and to Brother Angelo in Monte Casale. In the same manner they submitted themselves in obedience to a certain Brother Paul, the hermitage's cook.

Exhausted by the dust of the road and the fatigue of the past months, the brothers from Rome took their rest early. On the following morning they were roused from their beds by sounds at once unusual and most pleasant. Some of the brothers from Rome, more conversant with the spirituality of Brother Francis, thought at first that they were hearing that sweet and comforting melody which on one occasion had restored strength to Francis in his illness (LM 5:11), or if not that, then the melody of that noble falcon who had awakened him for the divine praises (2Cel 168). Others, however, relying more on their knowledge of zoology, immediately recognized that the sounds which had awakened them emanated from animals less noble, namely, from a large flock of hens, cocks, ducks, geese, and turkeys, which for some time now had come to share life with the brothers in the hermitage.

Not just on that first day but on all the following days, the brothers from Rome got out of bed to this music and made their way to the sanctuary to pray, bless the Lord, and to place all their cares in him (1Pt 5:7). Those brothers who already had been on pilgrimage to the Holy Places, remembering the sustained singing of birds on the wing, immediately gave this place the name of "San Pietro in Gallicanto" or "St. Peter at Cockcrow."

Under the maternal vigilance of the brothers of Emilia Romagna, the days following the musical awakening ran their course, full of creative intuitions. Brother Damian had conceived the idea of giving to each brother from Rome the name of a musical instrument; thus, one was called "Violin," another "Kettledrum," and another "German Flute." The result was that the brothers in their reflections began to pay special attention to music and to recommend it warmly to all the brothers scattered throughout the world as they strove to apply the Six-Year Plan adopted at the last Pentecost Chapter.

Basing their studies on Sacred Scripture and following the example of Brother Francis, they recognized with greater clarity than ever that in the contemplative dimension we should compare our own vocation to a melody which God himself suggests to each person, one which springs continuously from creation and from the human heart. This now becomes a means of giving thanks to God "for Himself" (RegNB 23:1), especially for God's "goodness, meekness, and beauty"(Adm 1) and for the harmony of creation. Filled with joy, the brothers from Rome realized that they formed one body with all their brothers and sisters among the animals, fowl, and birds, with whom Brother Francis had once recited the Divine Office (LM 8:9). Indeed the brothers became convinced in an altogether new manner that all creation is nothing other than polyphonic music to God, which they should accompany with their own voices. And that is precisely what they tried to do during those days in Monte Paolo in union with the cicada which, for the happiness of Francis, had sung all the praises of the Creator for eight full days (LM 8:9).

In the second priority of the Six-Year Plan, that of their option for the poor and, likewise, in their gospel witness in defense of justice and peace, the brothers ultimately realized that music is again an indispensable means. Was it not because of it that the bishop and the podestà [mayor] were reconciled once Francis had composed the musical stanza on reconciliation (LP 84)? Were there any means capable of breaking down in a peaceable manner the walls of hatred and injustice (2Cel 127) other than the "woody" violin of Brother Francis or the no less biblical trumpet of Jericho (Jos 6)? Or could the brothers have taken upon themselves in a credible manner the construction of a new heaven and a new earth if they had not been capable of listening with an attentive ear, as Francis did at Rieti in the poverty of his life, to the wonderful sound of the zither, whose music was so sweet and harmonious that "he thought he had been transported to another world" (LM 5:11; LP 66)?

Likewise, the preparation of a new kind of formation for the missionary spirit, the third Gospel priority of this large brotherhood, could never achieve success, as the brothers clearly recognized, without the knowledge of music. It was precisely here in Monte Paolo that they recalled the words of the Apostle Paul: "It is the same way with lifeless instruments that produce sound, such as a flute or a harp. If they do not give distinct notes, how will anyone know what is being played? And if the bugle gives an indistinct sound, who will get ready for battle" (1Cor 14:7-8)? In dark and cold England, in a place not far distant from learned

Oxford, as we read in a chronicle, a knight in armor approaching a t a gallop was converted to the Gospel at the sight of two Lesser Brothers who were walking barefoot in the snow, full of joy and singing the *Salve Regina* (*Lanercost Chronicle*).

Later on when Germany was divided into two provinces, one located in the region of the Rhine and the other in Saxony, was i t merely by accident that the general chapter itself placed at the disposal of the brothers psalters and antiphonaries for the chant, so as to raise the spirits of those tired missionaries on the other side of the Alps? (Giano 57). Finally, among the sisters and brothers in the groups known as basic ecclesial communities were there not perhaps many people worthy of mention, who in many ways fulfilled the word of the psalmist: "Sing to the Lord a new song"? (Ps 96:1) Was not Brother Francis himself a shining example of what is now known as inculturation? This is shown by the fact that even though he came from Umbria he knew how to sing in French (2Cel 90).

As the tranquil days in Monte Paolo drew to their close, the brothers were treated to a different artistic experience. Some of them even described it as a new and very intense form of up-to-the-minute "inculturation," one for which they had not yet found a model either in Sacred Scripture or in the life of Brother Francis. Brother Paul, the cook, choosing from among exquisite gifts of Mother Earth, over a period of months had reserved for the nutrition of the general council what might well be described as a crescendo in a symphony of eats and drinks. On the feast of Sts. Cosmas and Damian, also the feastday of the guardian of the hermitage, all the brothers were served a delicious meal as they recalled the words of Brother Francis, which stated that in time of necessity the brothers "may eat any ordinary food" (RegNB 9:13). Those brothers who were not accustomed to drinking wine or who drank very little now celebrated this festive banquet with an excellent wine called *Sangiovese*, one which has made the region of Monte Paolo famous. So they all ate and drank and had their fill. One brother, a native of the fogs of the north, realized too late that the day was Friday, a day on which it was forbidden to enjoy any kind of meat. He resolved to fast on another day.

On the evening of the same day, Brother Damian, the other brothers as well as Brother Berard, the minister of Bologna who had joined them, celebrated a solemn liturgy. During this the brothers from Rome, with the help of a sister, sang in parts some "psalms, hymns, and spiritual songs" (Col 3:16) as the Spirit inspired them. Under the influence of all that they had heard and seen, eaten, drunk, and talked about, the brothers from Rome sang in the manner which Francis desired: "The brothers should not pay any attention to the melody of the voice but rather to the harmony of the soul, so that the voice may be in unison with the soul, and the soul in unison with God. In this manner they may win God's favor by purity of heart while they are not trying to please the ears of the people by the sensuality of their voice" (EpOrd 6). However, the danger of such vain adulation did not, in fact, exist on that day.

In an impassioned homily Brother Damian warmly exhorted the general council to open their hearts to music, to sing together more frequently, and not to behave like the prisoners of Babylon, who hung up their harps on the willow trees and wept (Ps 137:1-2). Rather they should remember those other words which say: "May those who sow in tears reap with shouts of joy" (Ps 126:5). He added that in singing they should follow the example of their Father and Brother Francis, who on one occasion by means of insistent prayer stopped the diabolical noise of the demons on the roof of the church of Bovara, from where they were trying to terrorize him (2Cel 122). Brother Damian compared the brothers from Rome and from the whole world to an orchestra, in which the originality of each instrument contributes to the unity and harmony of the whole. Where there is noise, they should create silence and peace. Where there are discords and harsh sounds, they should create harmony and melodious song. Where too many soloists have entered the scene, they should form a choir or rather an orchestra.

After all these things the brothers left that hospitable hermitage. They felt comforted and consoled in their hearts because the Lord had shown them in a new way the task entrusted to them.

Monte Paolo, October 9, 1987

9. On how the Minister General of this brotherhood visited East Germany

Background: In November 1987 Minister General John Vaughn was able, together with H. Schalück, to pay an official visit to the former German Democratic Republic (East Germany). Thanks to a special permit, it was also possible for them to visit the pilgrimage center "Hülfensberg," which lay in the restricted border area.

Brother John and Brother Transalpinus, having solemnly celebrated the commemoration of their deceased brothers and sisters in the general curia on November 2, set out to visit that vice-province which is located in East Germany and is under the patronage of St. Francis himself. In this way they hoped to be edified by the spirit of the brothers there. By the time they reached Vienna, night was coming on. So they begged a certain Brother Ulric for a little refreshment and a bed on which to rest the night. Ulric gladly honored both requests.

The following morning these two pilgrims from Rome continued their journey towards the border which the local officials call the "European Peace Frontier" but which others call the "Iron Curtain." When they reached this frontier, the guards showed themselves so well disposed that they had no difficulty in getting permission to cross over to visit their brothers. After a brief stopover in Berlin, they were joined by Eusebius, the minister of the vice-province, who henceforth accompanied them everywhere. They all made what turned out to be a very worthwhile journey through cities and towns which even today give evidence of the conversion of the Saxon tribe, previously wild and ferocious, and of the implantation of our brotherhood in that tribe's territory.

They first reached Magdeburg where, according to trustworthy sources, a chapter of the seraphic Province of Saxony had already been celebrated in the year 1239 (Giano 69). Today, however, the friars have no foundation there. The local bishop was delighted that the brothers had come to pay him a visit and said that he wished the brothers would soon return to his city.

From there they went to Halberstadt, where the brothers had been sent as early as 1223 (Giano 36) and where an important chapter of the province had been held in 1262 (Giano, Prologue). To this day, thanks be to God, the brothers live there and announce the Gospel by word and deed. Here, as at the other stages of his journey, Brother John preached the word of God in admirable fashion and confirmed his brothers in the Christian way of life. Here too, as in other places, the solemn liturgy was enhanced by the pleasant voices of a choir and by the sound of instruments such as horns, trumpets, and flutes. Here as elsewhere, the celebrations were rounded off by the brothers partaking of a substantial banquet of "bread, milk, and eggs," as did the first brothers who had come from Italy to Germany (Giano 27)

In like manner they visited the cities of Dresden, Görlitz, and Bautzen, where they were kindly received by bishops and prelates, who gratefully accepted their greeting of peace and then instructed and informed the pilgrims on matters of great import for fraternal evangelization in the Diaspora, such as the so-called "Real Socialism" and other ideologies divorced from God. In the city of Bautzen they also celebrated a Eucharist and a fraternal meal with the Poor Clares, who in their convent of the Second Order in that country sing without ceasing the praises of the Most High.

When the two pilgrims and their guide and companion arrived at Halle, an extraordinary thing happened. Brother Andrew, the present guardian of Halle, had taken to his bed that very day, suffering from a severe attack of sciatica. At the fraternal and comforting greeting of Brother John, united to that of Brother Transalpinus, he suddenly felt himself free of pain, got up, and went about serving them. Later on, the Brother Minister exhorted all in his homily to continue living in the spirit of "discipline and austerity" which shone forth in the life of Brother Conrad of Brunsweig, who had been elected minister of Saxony during the the 1247 chapter celebrated in Halle (Giano 75).

By special favor of the powers-that-be in that country, the pilgrims were allowed to visit the shrine at Hülfensberg (Mount of Help), which is under the care of the friars and is dedicated to the memory of the Holy Cross and of St. Boniface. Since this mountain is under strict guard because of its proximity to the frontier, very few people are given permission to visit it. For that reason the brothers from Rome prayed here with intense fervor for peace in the hearts of all people and for the restoration of God's Kingdom of genuine justice for all, one which transcends the boundaries of language, race, ideologies, and systems. They prayed on the spot where, tradition says, the Apostle of Germany [Boniface] knocked down an oak tree dedicated to a pagan divinity.

In the fraternity of Dingelstädt the vice-province has its postulancy. Here Brother John declared himself as well as the worldwide brotherhood blessed because he was able to receive four young men as postulants. By this action he gave testimony that the life according to the Gospel and the *"forma vitae"* of our Father Francis can be subdued neither by power nor by violence.

A representative of the People of God presented Brother John with the gift reserved for guests: a long sausage. While making the presentation, the man said something which reveals the character of that tribe, "We are fond of long sausages and short sermons." So Brother John took the occasion to exhort the people and the friars, in a fairly short sermon, to allow the Gospel standards to take deep root in their hearts and in their culture. Finally, the Minister of all the brothers donated the sausage to the fraternity, particularly to the new novices, asking them to pray for the brothers who guide the Order and for their many responsibilities in such a way as to correspond with the quality and length of the sausage. Needless to relate, from that day forward many more prayers are said for the Minister and his councillors, for the blessing of all.

Finally, it is impossible not to make some reference to the other cultural and artistic stimuli which the brothers from the distant curia received. Actually, in their desire to open themselves to the dimension of music, which brings freedom and peace, and to make it helpful for the contemplative dimension, they visited Halle and Leipzig, two places consecrated to the memory of Georg Frideric Händel and of Johann Sebastian Bach. There the visitors allowed their hearts and emotions to be saturated with that music which seems to come directly from heaven and invites all people of goodwill to peace. Next they reached Eisenach, where shortly after the death of the Seraphic Father a certain Brother Herman von Weissensee had arrived and preached (Giano 41). There too is Wartburg Castle, world famous and consecrated to the memory of St. Elizabeth, daughter of the king of Hungary and wife of the landgrave of Thuringia. After the death of her husband, she lived under obedience to the Lesser Brothers (Chronicle of Salimbene 12). On the other hand, some centuries later, a certain Brother Martin Luther was forced to retire there for almost a year, in silence and penance, for having created difficulties for both the civil and religious authorities. During that year, however, he embarked on a most useful activity, namely, the translation of the Holy Scriptures into the simple language of the people.

In this place of Franciscan tradition, the brothers were wearing their habits. As they were coming down from the castle, they met a group of people who looked at them with surprise and asked them courteously whether they were "real friars" or "characters from some history play." With much simplicity but equal truthfulness they replied, "By the grace of God we are indeed real brothers of St. Francis, followers of the Poor Little Man of Assisi and subject to all." After having wished each other "Peace and All Good," both parties continued on their way.

The last stop made by the brothers was at Erfurt, exactly on the feast of St. Martin. Even to this day that city is well-known among the brothers because Brother Jordan of Giano himself had been sent there in the year 1224. The following year, so he reminds us in his

Chronicle, the friars went to live near the river "so as to be always able to wash their feet" (43). Erfurt is also famous because of Brother Nicholas, guardian of that city, whom Brother Albert of Pisa, then minister for the whole of Germany, tried to convince to accept the office of custos for Saxony. He initially refused to undertake this ministry, but after Brother Albert accused him of pride, he finally accepted it out of obedience. However, after accepting the office he found himself in such a dire condition that "he sang the Mass in ferial tone with a heavy heart" (49).

With thanksgiving for all that they had seen and heard, with a final greeting of peace at "the frontier of peace," and filled with confidence in the brotherhood of that region, Brother John and his companion returned to Rome.

Thuringia, November 17, 1987

10. How some brothers from Rome celebrated the advent of the Lord on African soil

Background: In December 1987 the author accompanied the Minister General and his secretary (Peter Williams) on a visit to the Ivory Coast and to Togo.

As the year of the Lord 1987 was coming to a close and while Sister Snow and Brother Wind were visiting the countries of Europe, lo there was heard in the place known as the curia of the Lesser Brothers the voice of one who called from beyond the desert of West Africa, "Brother John, come over . . . and visit us" (Acts 16:9). So it happened that the Minister and servant of the brothers set out in haste, bringing with him his secretary, Brother Peter, as well as Brother Transalpinus. On the wings of Brother Wind they flew towards that coast where many years ago ivory had been found. On the same day on which the Church of Rome began to intone the famous O Antiphons, they set out for another country called Togo.

While the three brothers traveled through the darkness of the African night, filled with the joy which characterizes the time preceding the feast of the birth of the Lord, they meditated upon the experiences of hospitality, fraternity, and "inculturation"—so it was called in those days—which the Lord would bestow on them on that continent.

And in their breviaries, which they always carried with them in accordance with a precept of their Rule, they found the words of

Scripture which opened their hearts and eyes to the meaning of some events which the Lord in his wisdom had prepared for them: "Be patient, therefore, beloved, until the coming of the Lord. The farmer waits for the precious crop from the earth, being patient with it until it receives the early and the late rains. You also must be patient. Strengthen your hearts, for the coming of the Lord is near" (Jas 5:7-8).

Enlightened and wonderfully consoled by these timely words, Brother John and his companions set foot on that continent and from then until the feast of the Nativity they traversed innumerable cities, villages, forests, and plains known there as savannas. Their purpose was to see and meet the brothers, to inform themselves on the growth and progress of the "Africa Project" as it is called, and what is more important, to allow their hearts to be touched and converted by the Gospel of Jesus.

First of all, the brothers from Rome were amazed and overjoyed by the hospitality showered on them wherever they went. On arrival at any place they would give and receive the greeting of Brother Francis: "The Lord give you peace." As they entered the churches and chapels of the various regions, they were covered with flowers by young girls who were both gracious and God-fearing. In the towns through which they passed, they were invited by the men, young and old, to take a seat beside them. Quite often they had the privilege of drinking delicious beer prepared in clay bowls from maize and millet. By way of contrast, on the occasion of another very opportune visit, an eminent cardinal of the Holy Roman Church gave them a drink which tasted very much as if it had come from distant Scotland. And again, on another courtesy call, a certain archbishop had killed a sheep in honor of his guests and offered them a delicious roast, seasoned with rare Spanish and French wine.

So the brothers praised the Lord, asking themselves whether such African hospitality might not be a sign of the Kingdom to come and yet already present, a prelude to that promised banquet of which rich and poor, Africans and Asians, Christians and Muslims, men and women of other faiths, prelates and simple friars will partake on an equal footing. And wherever the three brothers set foot, be it in some elegantly rich episcopal palace, built to receive the Lord Pope during his visit of a day and a half, in the huts of the natives, or in the simple dwellings of the friars, they constantly put into practice the words of Brother Francis, when he says: "Wherever they are and in whatever place the friars meet, they should treat one another in the spirit of love and mutual honor, without murmuring" (RegNB 7:15). Thus the brothers from Rome gave thanks to the Lord for this sign of the Kingdom of God.

Immediately the Brother Minister wished to be better informed on the progress of the "Africa Project" and of the implantation of the brotherhood in those regions. For that purpose he and his companions visited all those fraternities into which, after long years of "drought," many brothers from different tribes, nations, and languages had been received. These wished to come to know our form of life and to follow the Gospel, the Rule, and the third priority of the Six-Year Plan. In all those places Brother John celebrated a fraternal Eucharist with the candidates, explaining to each and all the commandment received from the Lord, namely, that they should be the pioneers of an inculturated brotherhood, at once international and intercultural, in which all are called to be brothers and sisters under the one Lord; also that they should bestow on the universal brotherhood and on the Church those values which are characteristic of the African continent: authentic "minority" and that sense of family in which mutual respect, maternal charity, and fraternal co-responsibility hold sway (RegB 6). In all these meetings and reunions, celebrated in various languages but in one sole spirit, everyone became aware that Africa was not so much a project of the Order as a gift and project of God for the Order, designed to inculcate in and to recall to the Order its catholic and apostolic character, granting it the gift of renewed and committed young members.

The African brothers, on their part, taught the brothers from Rome a proverb which says, "If you believe in the future, plant a tree." So while there arose from venerable curial churches of Rome the sound of the solemn and vibrant antiphon, "O Radix Jesse," the Minister General of all the brothers decided that, as a sign of his determination to implant the brotherhood in a new and lasting way on African soil, he would plant in the brothers' garden various trees—palms and hibiscus among others.

Meanwhile Brother Peter and Brother Transalpinus had to be content with planting smaller and less imposing, but no less useful, shrubs. Since it was the month of December and still a time of drought, they watered the plants generously, conscious of that other Gregorian melody which is customarily sung in Rome, "Drop down dew, ye heavens." In addition, with a view to representing better the "Africa Project" to the brothers, the Brother Minister decided to write an encyclical letter which should bear the name of another African proverb—"In order to encircle the baobab tree, many hands are needed." So all the brothers gave thanks to the Lord also for this sign of the Kingdom.

In short, the visitors had ample motives for meditating on the word "inculturation," much used by theologians of that epoch. In all humility they were anxious to know what its meaning might be. And the Lord led them through one of those great parks where, according to the vision of the prophet, elephants, monkeys, lions, and gazelles lived together in peace (Is 11:6-8), and where they pick up snakes which would not harm them (Mk 16:18).

So they finally came upon the tribe of the Moba in the north of the country where a well had been sunk. A crowd of people with many animals had united for the purpose of saluting Sister Water, always welcome in these regions. A priest, a son of the tribe, blessed the water and explained that water is the origin of all life, that which causes the desert to bloom and the savanna to shoot forth an abundance of precious crops, maize and millet especially. Then he related the conversation between Jesus and the woman at the well of Samaria (Jn 4:5-42) and spoke about that water which, according to the word of the Lord Jesus, can satisfy all thirst, the water by which we must be reborn. Having said all this, the priest told a woman who carried a child on her back to take water from the well for the first time. He then blessed the water and with it sprinkled both people and animals. All present, whether Christians, Muslims, animists, catechumens, or friars, admired this timely method of evangelization, known to some brothers in those days as "liberating and integral evangelization."

Both in their meeting with the Poor Clare Sisters in the capital and in their visits to numerous outstations, the brothers felt especially moved by the beauty of the instruments and of the African melodies and dances, to the point of temporarily forgetting the Roman melodies. Full of spiritual contentment, they allowed themselves to be carried away by these dance rhythms.

In yet another capital the brothers had the privilege of celebrating the solemn Eucharist of the birth of the Lord, this time embellished by the Gregorian melodies and by other Christmas carols brought to these shores some one hundred years ago by German missionaries. These were so familiar to Brother Transalpinus that to his pleasant surprise he was able to sing with his brother Africans all through Christmas night the carols of his beloved Saxony. Tied to the Crib were two sheep and a goat. For everybody's edification, neither did these remain silent. They finally ceased to bleat only when they had been solemnly incensed by Brother John! Thus everyone recalled that night in Greccio when Brother Francis, full of tenderness for the humanity of God, had represented for the first time in history, the birth of Jesus, poor and suffering, in the midst of his people (lCel 84-86; 2Cel 199). Thus all gave thanks to God for this sign of his coming.

Having come to the end of their pilgrimage, the brothers from the general curia realized that had come to some new awarenesses, namely:

- that the same seed of the Gospel and the form of evangelical life of Brother Francis should be planted in all the continents. However, its fruits will always be varied and distinct, producing rich tastes and odors according to time, place, and temperature in zones which in Rome are still called "peripheral";
- that according to the wise words of the Lord Pope Paul VI (*Evangelii Nuntiandi*), the evangelizer must first of all be evangelized;
- that the Lord is always present when two, three or more people or nationalities are united in his name (Mt 18:20) in one fraternity in order to plant the Gospel and cause Jesus to be born in today's world;
- that all races, tribes, tongues, religions, and cultures can find a common ground in those fundamental values which the Lord instills in all people and which make possible an authentic inculturation in accordance with the Gospel, namely, mutual respect, love for life, and for all creation, hospitality, and the desire for peace.

So the brothers gave thanks to the Lord for these intuitions as well as for his presence among all men and women of goodwill.

The Brother Minister and his companions returned to Rome by the same way as they had set out. They landed at the city called holy and eternal on the feast of St. Stephen, enriched with spiritual gifts, interiorly purified, and knowing that their African brothers had confided to them the wisdom of a local proverb which says: "Mother dear, carry me on your back. When you are old, I will carry you."

                                    Rome, January 1, 1988

1988

11. How the Plenary Council of the fraternity, meeting in India, strove to deepen its understanding of these words of wisdom, "Light from the East"

Background: *A plenary council is an important meeting of the Order between general chapters. In Bangalore, India, some seventy friars from throughout the world met in May 1988 to review the life of the worldwide brotherhood.*

After the Pentecost Chapter which took place in the Portiuncula in the year of our Lord 1985, 1001 days and nights had come and gone in Rome when, lo, from hills and valleys all over the world, and from the five continents, over land and from the sky, the brothers came together in Krishnajarapura near Bangalore, India. They gathered out of obedience to a venerable custom, enshrined now as a rule of the new General Constitutions (193-195), which refers to celebration of the Plenary Council of the Order.

Mindful of their mission of advancing the work of inculturation (GC 92) and the evangelization of cultures (GC 94), the brothers had decided to hold this important meeting in the mysterious land of India. Many undertook the difficult journey with the secret expectancy that, faced with so many problems which weigh upon the worldwide brotherhood, they might have a profound experience of those hope-filled words, *"Ex Oriente Lux"* (light from the East).

On the vigil of the feast of St. Joseph the Worker, a large number of ministers met in Krishnajarapura, in a seminary belonging to the sons of Don Bosco, because the Lesser Brothers of the Province of St. Thomas in that country live in houses which are poor and simple. When the brothers from all over the world arrived at that seminary which is called *Kristu Yoti*, they were filled with holy joy on learning that *yoti*, in one of the many languages of that country, is the word for *light*. In fact, it was the light of Christ for which they were all searching; and it was a torch kindled with this light that they all ardently desired to bring back to their own places.

With the love of brothers and mothers, the sons and daughters of that immense country devoted themselves to caring for the friar-pilgrims with a smile always hovering on their lips. The friars themselves remained almost a whole month in that part of the Indian subcontinent. There they learned that before undertaking the evangelization of cultures and religions, they must first listen to what the Lord God graciously wishes to reveal to them by means of those cultures and those religions. This helps every fraternity to come ever closer to the Gospel and become more credible in its catholicity.

Tired from such a long journey the brothers retired early to enjoy a refreshing sleep. The real life lessons which they were called upon to learn during the following weeks began on that very first night—lessons all the more enlightening and surprising insofar as they were not the result of lively debates and subtle reasonings about the rules for conducting a Plenary Council. Instead they were the fruit of a new encounter with nature, religions, and cultures, without forgetting the brothers and sisters of that vast country.

The encounter with nature took place during that night or rather at the crack of dawn with the cawing of Brother Crow looking for food (Ps 147:9) and the lowing of their sisters, the sacred cows, which were happily grazing around the house. Those members of the brotherhood who had come from cold climates were not a little surprised at the multitude of small creatures which shared the same cell with them and filled the place with a sheer variety of sounds. There were ants, frogs, reptiles, locusts, and mosquitoes, all eager to feed on Brother Friar. The brothers who had come from the so-called developed countries very quickly asked for insecticides, all set for chemical warfare without mercy.

It was then that Brother Fidelis, minister of the fraternity in India, smiled in his most brotherly way and proceeded to impart his first lesson: "True to a tradition at once Brahmanic, Hindu, and Franciscan, we ought to harbor sentiments of peace towards all creatures, including those little beasts which may appear unintelligent and useless." He based this statement on GC 71 which says that "the friars are to maintain a reverent attitude towards nature, threatened from all sides today, in such a way that they may restore it completely to its condition of brother." He appealed to them to allow the hard-working ants to continue their laborious activity—what a good example for everyone!—and to carry the other little creatures out to the garden if their company should prove a burden. Finally, to the surprise of some, he sowed in the hearts of the brothers the seed of a sutra of Patanjali, the celebrated author of aphorisms on yoga: "He who is a firm believer in nonviolence creates around himself an atmosphere of peace which disarms the violence of all who come near him" (II Sutra 35).

Some of the brothers who like to think that Francis had come to India in some mysterious way immediately went leafing through the Franciscan sources to see if they could find any point of contact with that country so full of mystery and so rich in traditions. Their professional investigation lead them to a sermon by Jacques de Vitry (1180-1240), a good friend of the early friars. In 1240 this cardinal preached to the brothers his sermon on the Book of Proverbs (30:24-28): "Four things on earth are small, yet they are exceedingly wise: the ants are a people without strength, yet they provide their food in the summer; the badgers are a people without power, yet they make their home in the rocks; the locusts have no king, yet all of them march in rank; the lizard can be grasped with the hand, yet it is found in kings' palaces."

The preacher compared the brothers to these creatures. The friars who are unselfish workers and feel obliged always to seek the good of others, particularly that of the weak, are the ants. The friar who is not ashamed of his weakness but places his confidence in the help he receives from others, especially from the Lord, the true rock—he is the badger. The brothers who have received from God the gift of building the Christian community and who make great strides thanks to study and contemplation—these are the locusts. Finally, the indefatigable itinerant preachers who distribute the bread of God's word among the People of God—these are to be compared to the lizards who are to be found in the palaces of kings.

The brothers gave thanks to the Lord for these lively instructions, which helped them understand their mission in a new way. Had not Brother Francis, indeed, shown the greatest respect for all creatures, including the very smallest and those apparently deprived of reason? (1Cel 58; SalVirt; LP 110). And was not Christ Jesus himself the model of all inculturation, born on the periphery, far from the center of the Roman empire, among the animals and among the poor?

The meeting with other religions also brought with it a harvest of new experiences. To the brothers convened in Kristu Yoti college, the Lord gave such confidence in their Hindu brothers that they went one day to visit an ashram. They asked a swami, who was dressed in his sari, to speak to them about his great master, Sri

Ramakrishna, about his love for all creation, about his radical poverty and the way that leads to illumination. To their great surprise they learned that, like Francis, the elder brother of Ramakrishna had despised money and had thrown it far away from him (2Cel 65); similarly the Hindu monk had trodden it underfoot and, as if it were no more than the dirt of the street, thrown it into the Ganges. On the banks of the sacred river he had cried out: "If at any time I should have money in my hand, may it wither and may my breathing fail."

Thereupon the swami told them of a disciple who wished to put the great master to the test. One day when Ramakrishna was not in his cell, the disciple placed a coin beneath his mat. When the master returned and sat on his mat, he let out a cry of pain. It was as if an arrow had pierced him. He looked around him bewildered, unable to find an explanation. Then the disciple came in and saw his guru. At the same time, a servant entered and found the silver coin beneath the mat.

These meetings and anecdotes had quite an effect on the brothers, even to the point of confusing them. On the one hand, they thought of the preferential option for the poor, which they had so joyfully embraced and, on the other, of the financing of the general curia and of other houses which the brotherhood has in Rome.

In the city of Mysore the brothers paid a visit to a second ashram, one maintained by a son of St. Ignatius and so, a most catholic one. There they celebrated the Eucharist resting on their haunches, according to local tradition. There were many reverences, flowers, and much incense in an atmosphere of strange words and exotic chants. During a homily the Indian priest invited the brothers to deepen their vocation in an Asiatic context. "In accordance with Hindu tradition," he said, "the thought process of Francis is more associative than logical, more intuitive than analytical, more subjective than objective, more inductive than deductive, especially if one compares his thought with the reasoning processes of western scholasticism." With great patience the Christian guru explained to the brothers that the true liberation theology of the East is the fruit of a pure interior and of contemplation. It springs up from within and overflows onto the poor and suffering. However, it always tries to appear before the Goodness of God with empty hands.

At this the brothers never ceased to give thanks to the Lord for the communion of saints of all the religions of the world. Neither did they cease to marvel at the words written by the Indian poet

Rajjib some four centuries ago: "All the religions of the world are like streams which flow into God, the only Ocean."

Among many meetings with local brothers and sisters which were a means of evangelization for the brothers of the plenary council, allow me to mention the visit of one brother of St. Francis, a man called Dayanand, dressed in a sari. His manner of living was based on that of the Hindu monks. Like a *sannyasi*, he lived with the poor in an attitude of absolute nonviolence *(ahimsa)*, the kind which our brother Mahatma Gandhi had displayed before the whole world. Brother Dayanand gave a description of *sannyasi* in accordance with the *Treatise of the Equivalents*:

"Free as a infant newly-born, without any ties to property, place yourselves resolutely on the road of Brahman. With purity of heart and as a means of sustaining a languishing life, fill the receptacle of your stomach with the alms which you receive. Whether you receive something or absolutely nothing, always maintain an unchanging disposition. You may live in an abandoned house, in a temple, in the shade of a tree or in an abandoned anthill, among the roots of a tree or in a potter's cabin, beside a bivouac or in the sand of a riverbed, on a hill or in a cave, in the cavity of a tree or beside a waterfall, or finally, on the bare earth with no cover. Without self pity, without constraint or tension, in an attitude of deep contemplation, and concentrating on the great YES, you should apply yourselves to facing the consequences of evil actions in the past, abandoning yourselves to renunciation" *(Jabala Upanishad* 6).

These words reminded them of the life of Francis. The brother also referred to the life of the imprisoned Gandhi, who would continue to repeat: "The disciple of nonviolence is never afraid. Although his enemy may deceive him twenty times, he is ready to trust the twenty-first time."

On hearing such things the brothers gave thanks to the Lord for the many delicious fruits still growing on the tree of Franciscan living. Those who were most grateful were the brothers who have dedicated themselves in a special manner to the Gospel priority of peace and justice and have suffered contradictions of all kinds. These felt very consoled and encouraged by such a testimony.

After the brothers had studied and deepened their knowledge of "the things of God" (RegNB 18:1), after their encounters with the nature, the culture, and the religions of that country, it was easy for them to enter upon the themes which they had chosen while still in their beautiful, spacious house in Rome.

In the light of their experience, they renewed their commitment to live out the priorities of their Six-Year Plan, namely:

- to taste the sweetness of contemplation, even by adopting new forms of prayer more in keeping with today's religious sensitivity (GC 29);
- to become fearless defenders of peace and justice, overcoming evil by the practice of good (GC 68:1);
- to be heralds of the Gospel in word and deed by promising to seek out new forms of living the Franciscan charism (GC 115:2).

They decided to begin renewal in their houses of studies along the lines of the encyclical of the Lord Pope, *Sollicitudo Rei Socialis*, by putting these at the service of the evangelization of cultures and of listening to the voice of the poor. They would not neglect, however, the *"Sollicitudo Rei Medievalis,"* which in the opinion of some should be given a new impulse, especially in Rome.

As regards finances, they decided to put into practice not only a more equitable system of contributions in favor of the curia but also a more radical sharing with the poor. All provinces without distinction were invited to adopt this.

Before concluding, we must not fail to mention the fact that the day before the departure of the brothers, just as they had joyously made a synthesis of their new projects and plans in the format of *A Message From Bangalore* to be the ripe fruit of their stay in India, lo and behold, the well ran dry, the well which had served the needs of all the brothers and of the sons of Don Bosco alike! For half a day, beneath a broiling sun, they suffered severe thirst and were unable to perform their customary ablutions. Then they began to pray to the Lord in the words of the psalm which says: "My soul thirsts for you, my flesh faints for you, as in a dry and weary land, where there is no water" (Ps 63:1). They solemnly promised for the future to follow Brother Francis in all cultures with a pure heart, limpid eyes, and a great openness of spirit (Ex 15:22-25). And behold, the spring of water began to fill the well. All saw in this a sign of the goodness of the Lord, who is constantly testing the brothers only to bless promptly all their efforts at renewal.

Refreshed and purified interiorly and exteriorly, the ministers and the brothers returned from the Plenary Council, some to Rome, others to their home countries, convinced that the Lord had shown them once more what was expected of them. They were grateful for that light which they had seen in the East and which had guided them on their way.

Assisi, August 8, 1988

12. How the provincial ministers of Europe, gathered in Verona, were enlightened by a word of God which says: "Some take pride in chariots, some in horses, but our pride is in the name of the Lord our God" (Ps. 20:7)

Background: For the first time in recent history, in October 1988, all the ministers provincial of Europe came together in Verona in order to reflect on the contribution of the Franciscan Order in a Europe at that time still divided.

When in the month of October in the year of the Lord 1988, the Lord Pope, John Paul II, had gone to the European Parliament in Strasbourg in order to call the nations of the ancient continent to conversion and to a new evangelization, it also happened that the provincial ministers of almost all the Provinces of Europe, of East and West, were holding a reunion with a view to giving testimony once again of their obedience to the Holy See and of making their contribution, in customary humility, to the unity and the evangelization of their divided continent. This meeting was the first of its kind ever held. The place chosen for it was the splendid city of Verona, in the north of the Italian peninsula. It was here that Brother Francis long ago learned with great sorrow that the brothers of Bologna had become concerned about their own comfort rather than about salutary poverty and had built a large house. This Francis commanded them to abandon promptly (2Cel 58).

The ministers convened in Verona burned with ardent zeal for their seraphic Father and Brother. Obedient to the signs of the times, they strove to understand the meaning of the "common house" of all the peoples, tribes, and nations of Europe. They held discussions on the kind of foundations on which this common house could be built and what kind of contribution towards its construction could be made by the poor men of Assisi, men rich indeed in the gifts and charisms which Francis had bequeathed to them.

When the brothers arrived at the large, well-built residence to which Brother Augustinus Venetus had invited them—which, of course, happily belonged to the local bishop—their joy was full to overflowing. In spite of the frontiers and walls which today prevent the continent from reaching its proper stature, only three brothers had been unable to follow the Lord Pope's urging. They had failed to obtain from the powerful of this world the necessary safe-conduct passes. It was but a short time previously that the rulers of the East had begun speaking in guarded terms about "perestroika" and "glasnost." Within the brotherhood, however, openness and frankness had never been lacking. In fact, had not our Brother Francis firmly commanded all his sons and daughters that they should have no hesitation in making known their needs to one another? (RegB 6:8). Under the protection of their Venetian host, the brothers joyfully applied themselves to work, prayer, and fraternal recreation, which often did not end until well into the deep night and occasionally continued until the hour of Matins.

In the first stage of what surely were deep reflections, the stage called **look**, the brothers gave time to the exchange of information. Each one spoke of his own country, of its political system, of living conditions, the nature of their work and witness. Then they shared their hopes and fears concerning the construction of this "European house." Before coming to Verona each one had prepared a list of his brothers and the houses in which they lived. Having made a quick calculation on their fingers, they discovered that more than half the brothers worldwide were living in Europe, that is, 11,000 friars.

They discussed what they ought to do towards their renewal in view of the third millennium, in order to live the Gospel of Christ in a manner which seemed credible to a secularized society and, insofar as it depended on them, inject a new fraternal sap into the old, somewhat dry trunk of the Church and the Order on their continent.

With honest sincerity and with the help of theology and the human sciences, they sought to find their place in the modern world. So they took up the study of the important themes of the moment: action and contemplation, the mystical and the political, being and having, light and darkness, Rome and Assisi, first world and third, East and West, socialism and capitalism, theory and practice, Martha and Mary, Francis and Clare, yin and yang, transalpine and cisalpine brothers, clerics and laics, mission and evangelization, sensibility and solidarity, order and fraternity, Church and Kingdom of God.

When the brothers had been wholly immersed in plans for the future and statistics, they decided to have a well-earned rest. They went on cultural excursions to discover that complementarity and bipolarity of which the continent seems to be full. They found the perfume of Juliet which was capable of attracting the attention of Romeo and whose pleasant remembrance is preserved in Verona to this day.

Having **looked** for the space of three days, the brothers then began to **judge**. For this purpose they had invited a prince of the Church of Rome who lives in a country under the Southern Cross, a certain Brother Aloysius of Fortaleza. They had chosen him because this Brother Cardinal is a fervent advocate of the renewal of the Church starting out from the viewpoint of the poor. They also invited him because the European brothers who were preparing for the celebration of the fifth centenary of the evangelization of America in 1992 desired that a representative of the young Churches of the New World should come to stimulate them in their preparations. The brothers from Europe wished to understand better the role which their continent had played in the "discovery" of peoples—a role which the peoples who had been "discovered" often called an "invasion"—and what might be the brothers' role in the future. Above all they wished to know what the Lord desired of them at this decisive moment in history and, if it should be necessary, to "do penance with the blessing of God" (Test 26).

With ardent fearlessness and gentle brotherliness, Brother Aloysius invited the European ministers to sound the depths of their conscience. "There is need for humility and courage," said the prelate. "Humility, because the operation mounted by the European brothers relied a great deal more on their 'chariots and horses' and not nearly enough on 'the name of the Lord'" (Ps 20:8). "Your peoples," continued the cardinal, "relied more on a 'culture of having' than on a 'culture of being and of fraternity.' The people of the so-called first and second worlds ought, in the name of Christ's love, to cease building their well-being on the sweat of the poor of the so-called third and fourth worlds. For unless there is justice at the planetary level, there will be no peace in Europe. However, the brothers of Europe too ought to have the courage to rediscover their most authentic values; they should return to the ideal of liberty, equality, and fraternity, trying to embellish this ideal with the colors of minority and a sense of familiarity which Brother Francis left them as an inheritance. They should fearlessly take a stand in matters of peace, justice, and the protection of our sister and mother, Earth. They ought to establish communion with the old poor and the new poor, always, however, meditating on those wise words coming from the Orient: 'Before correcting others, first make the round of your own house three times.' When ancient Europe observes these things and seeks first and foremost the Kingdom of God and his justice in economics, culture, politics, and—lest we forget it—in theology and spirituality; when above all it is mindful of the *kenosis* of Jesus, our Lord, then it will be filled to the brim with the blessings of heaven, and all things else will be added: hope, a future, and a renewed youth," concluded the Brother Cardinal.

Thus enlightened and encouraged in the midst of a concert of voices and languages which burst forth in prayer and praise of the glory of the Lord of History, the ministers went on to the stage of **action** and to the laying of the first humble stones for the construction of a new, Franciscan Europe. So they decided on the following:

- A meeting in 1992, not to celebrate a triumphalist commemoration of the "discovery" of America but to organize a penitential celebration by way of preparation for a new and deeper evangelization of Europe;
- The promotion of significant initiatives in the fields of justice, peace, and the protection of the environment all over the continent; they would urge the leaders of East and West to open wide their frontiers, renouncing forever any recourse to "chariots and horses" and all other instruments of war;
- Formation of young friars in an attitude of openness to other cultures and foreign languages since Brother Francis had given the example when he spoke in French as well as in Italian (LM 2:5).

A group of seven brothers, representing the seven major regions of Europe, was commissioned to "coordinate and animate" dialogue among the brothers of the continent. So great was this group's desire to come together again that they arranged to meet in Cologne, near the tomb of Duns Scotus. This genuine universal brother was a native of Scotland and taught at Oxford in the country of the Angles, Jutes, and Saxons as well as at Paris; he died in Lower Germany, where he rests in peace.

In his closing homily Brother Aloysius exhorted all the brothers to construct a "new house" which would be pleasing to Francis. Its foundation and cornerstone would be the Lord Jesus himself (Eph 2:20); its stout pillars would be the evangelical priorities of the last Pentecost Chapter; its door would be hospitality and its roof, courtesy, which is the companion of God

and the sister of love (Fior 37; 2Cel 86). Brother Aloysius hoped
and prayed that this house would be open to all and that its
cloister would embrace the whole world (SC 63).

In the midst of prayer and thanksgiving which rose up
unceasingly to heaven, one could hear the accents of languages
native to European minorities: Maltese, Ruthenian, Gaelic, Breton,
Basque, Catalan, Slovene, Latin, and Albanian among others—an
obvious sign that all, without distinction and with equal dignity,
belonged to one sole family.

And they said goodbye with the words of a song by Dom Helder
Camara:

> If you dream alone, your dream remains a dream,
> If you dream with others, something new is born.

Then each one set out for his province, feeling comforted and
grateful for all that God's inexhaustible mercy had graciously
revealed to them.

Verona, October 1988

13. How the fruits of the Spirit (Gal 5:22) were distributed to the
directors of novices of our brotherhood assembled in Assisi

*Background: In October-November 1988 there took place in Assisi a
congress of all the novice directors of the Order. The main points
and the results of this meeting are presented in the following text,
using a variety of symbols.*

In the year of our Lord 1988, three years after the Pentecost
Chapter and two years after the approval of the new General
Constitutions by the Lord Pope, the Minister General of this
brotherhood, together with the body called the general council,
decided to call the attention of the brotherhood to Chapter VI of
the General Constitutions. This chapter deals with the formation
of the brothers and, faithful to the intention and the words of our
Father and Brother, Francis, bears the title, "To Have the Spirit of
the Lord" (RegB 10:8). It appeared more important than ever to
help the brothers from many parts of the world to rediscover the
spirit of the Lord and his holy operation in their lives, doing so
more by the testimony of their lives than by means of documents
and clever writings, by induction rather than by deduction, by
practice rather than by theory, by means of the Gospel rather than
by human laws, there in Assisi rather than in Rome.

The Minister of all the masters of novices of the universal brotherhood called them to a meeting in the Domus Pacis in Assisi. The work of preparing this meeting and of bringing it to a successful conclusion fell to Brothers Sebastian and Saul, with the aid of several others. So shortly after the feast of the Transitus of Francis, our Father and Brother, one hundred and eight Masters from fifty countries gathered in the Portiuncula not so much to talk in abstract terms about formation as to be filled themselves with the Spirit of the Lord and of our Brother Francis. They sought to bring forth fruits of penance and conversion under the influence of that same Spirit. During four weeks they tried to discern the signs of God in their lives, allowing themselves to be evangelized by prayer and work—in Assisi, at La Verna, in the valley of Rieti, and on the holy island of Lake Trasimene.

Here then are the sacred signs and symbols by means of which the Spirit of the Lord spoke to the brotherhood in a novel manner according to the spirit of Francis and of the new General Constitutions. It is a report which one of the participants wrote in few and simple words.

The *Tau* or the fruit of ongoing conversion

At the beginning of their labors Brother Minister John handed each one a wooden Tau, a sign of election and salvation and so dear to the heart of Francis that he used it to sign his letters (LM prol. 2). Then those who previously had found the task of imparting formation to others bitter because their work was difficult and unsuccessful—to be compared to that of the sower who had scattered the seed on rocky ground (Mt 13:5)—joyfully wore this Tau night and day. In a remarkable way this sign restored their courage and confidence. They came to realize that they could not apply themselves to the formation of others unless they had first allowed themselves to be made Christ's own (Phil 3:12). They became more aware of the significance of the Tau and of the importance it had for Francis; they now understood how to read his life from a new perspective. Above all, they understood that there exists no more important pedagogical principle than a life which reveals their likeness to Christ (Gal 4:19), a life which derives its dynamism from the radiating force of personal witness.

Some of those who before had wondered how little fruit they had derived from their studies of pedagogy, psychology, and group therapy suddenly discovered, as if by a new insight, the principles which Francis himself—the only genuine model of Minors—had embodied. Had he not stated that it was not a question of books and theories, no matter how useful they might be, including theology? What mattered was the capacity to be an instrument of the Spirit of the Lord and a witness to his holy operation (RegB 10:8; EpAnt 2). Had not Brother Francis preferred to every other book, the cross of Christ, the "book" which he read day and night without fail (LM 4:3)?

The more the friar masters extended their stay in Assisi and the more they reflected on the mission which the Lord had confided to them, the more deeply they entered into peace with themselves. The words of Thomas Merton, who was himself a novice master, came to their minds and hearts: "We do not experience conversion only once in a lifetime, but several times. And this continuous repetition of little and great conversions, of interior turmoil, leads us on to one only Metanoia, our becoming transformed into the image of Christ." Renewed in mind, they all decided to imitate their Father and Brother Francis, about whom they read: "Day by day the blessed Francis was being filled with consolation and the grace of the Holy Spirit, as with ever greater care and vigilance, he continued the formation of his new sons by means of new instructions, teaching them to walk with sure step along the road of holy poverty and of blessed simplicity" (1Cel 26).

That was the first fruit of the Assisi meeting.

The *guitar* or happiness in God

Nobody doubts the difficulty of the work of personal conversion according to the "form of Christ" and the need for asceticism on the part of one whose work is forming others. Nevertheless, just as Francis at a time of his very severe asceticism and piercing sufferings had been consoled by heavenly music (LP 24; LM 5:11), so now, centuries later, his brothers did not wish to be deprived of that consolation which is imparted by the melody of their own voices and the harmony of instruments, old and new. They too wanted to have an experience of the creative spirit of the Lord of music. Many had brought their instruments with them: guitars and flutes, horns and fifes, violins and ten-stringed harps, cymbals and drums, trumpets and bandores, oboes and clarinets, cornets and lyres.

A certain Brother Ivo from Dalmatia sounded forth on the great organ and accompanied the Gregorian chant while Brother

Marino of Fonte Colombo, a place where Francis "composed" the Rule, conducted the choir in church. Not only did the brothers sing solemnly during the divine liturgies, they also sang during the multinational and multicultural recreations which took place in a venerated aula adorned with ancient frescoes in the convent of the Portiuncula. This same hall was the one which had frequently been used throughout history for the Pentecost Chapters. With the sound of music the Spirit of the Lord wished to reveal their mission to them. St. Ignatius of Antioch had a way of expressing it very harmoniously. Should they not consider their vocation as a "melody engraved in their minds by God?" As they now perceived more clearly than ever, could they not make of their lives a fitting example in the work of formation of their friars, when "By the rivers of Babylon—there we sat down and there we wept when we remembered Zion. On the willows there we hung up our harps" (Ps 137:1-2)? Was it not a matter of interpreting their own history and their personal vocation as a voice in the midst of a polyphonic chorus which sang the praises of creation before the Lord of life?

In the area of formation, was it not a matter of intoning a "new song" (Ps 40:4)—as Brother Armando from distant Colombia so aptly observed in his conference on minority and work, a matter of a more radical life-style in the midst of the poor? And that fraternity in which and for which we live—does it not resemble a choir or an orchestra in which the various talents are so many different instruments but in which mutual listening and attention to the one and only Lord (Mt 23:8) combine to avoid cacophony?—as Brother John Baptist from Gaul never tired of repeating. Does not that diversity of talents-instruments, placed at the service of overall harmony, help towards building up the Kingdom of God? And the varied timbre of voices, the use of diverse instruments, old and new, in the execution of one single symphony, are not these an obvious symbol of the pluriformity of charism which Brother Francis has bequeathed to us? Should not formators and masters be gifted with a finely tuned ear to help them discern the melody which the Lord both of music and of history has engraved in the person of every novice?

As often happen in places steeped in sanctity, the brothers united in Assisi were wonderfully enlightened and came to understand clearly that their charism was missionary and that they were sent forth to give concerts not only in cells, churches, and chapels, but as Brother Leo from Indonesia recalled, also on the six continents. So by way of affirming their vocation of "not living for themselves alone but for others," on one cold evening they set out with their bizarre instruments and their repertoire of songs for the Piazza del Comune of Assisi. There they sang, danced, and played their instruments until late into the night for the glory of God and the edification of the people. And all who saw and heard them were extremely amazed at the enduring vigor and the formative creativity of the Franciscan life.

All the brothers were overjoyed at this second fruit of the Assisi meeting.

The *rock* or the foundation of our fraternity

During a liturgy that was as festive as it was fraternal in the peaceful hermitage of San Damiano—that same place in which the formation of Francis took a decisive turn—the minister of the fraternity in Umbria gave each one a small stone, symbol of another fruit of the Spirit. It is not difficult to describe to what kind of knowledge or experience this concrete symbol was meant to relate. In the precious writings which they were studying night and day, the masters had read how Francis at the beginning of his conversion had carried heavy stones (LM 2:7); how he had walked respectfully on stones out of consideration for him who is the living stone (2Cel 165); how he venerated holy poverty as the foundation stone of the brotherhood (Fior 13; SC prol.); how he came to look upon his sickness and tribulations as if they were precious stones (LP 83); how "he raised up the noble edifice of charity, in which living stones, gathered from all corners of the world, formed the temple of the Holy Spirit" (lCel 38); how the Order always and everywhere is built up solely by observing the Gospel (LM 3:8); and how Francis from the beginning of his conversion had like a wise architect based his life and that of his Order only on the highest humility and poverty of the Son of God (LP 9).

The unimportant stone from San Damiano thus became for the formators the cornerstone on which to base their formation work. In their act of thanksgiving the novice masters promised, with a clearer and more consistent commitment than ever, to contribute by their work to the building up of a renewed brotherhood. Several acknowledged that it should lead to inculturation and insertion among the poor who are our teachers (Bahia 41). Also, that it should lead those brothers whom the Lord sends us to contemplate the mystery of God, starting with the viewpoint of the poor.

When they had spent some time discussing the issue of an

"open" novitiate or a "closed" one, they looked upon the stone of San Damiano as an invitation to remain always open to the experience of the fruits of the Spirit, open above all to the God revealed in the poor. Every fraternity which is built upon the foundation of the poor Christ—as the friars coming from the younger Churches and provinces did not fail to recall—should personally experience what the Prophet Isaiah describes: "Enlarge the space for your tent, spread out your tent cloths unsparingly; lengthen your ropes and make firm your stakes. For you shall spread abroad to the right and to the left; your descendants shall dispossess the nations and shall people the desolate cities" (Is 54:2-3).

There now was the third fruit of the Assisi meeting.

The *grain of wheat* or evangelization of one's own heart

At the closing of this memorable meeting, when all were about to hurry back to their countries, a departure liturgy was celebrated in which Brother John gave to each one a grain of wheat, symbol of the word of God which always desires to fall on good soil (Mt 13; Lk 8; Mk 4), also a symbol of a new life (Jn 12:24), and finally a reminder that all evangelization must first take root in one's own heart. On that day there was no homily. Instead, each one received in his hand a grain of wheat and then began to speak to his heart.

Can one come to know life according to the Gospel if not by means of a journey which becomes a faithful following of Christ (Adm 7)? Can a master be other than a disciple of Christ (Phil 2:7)? Can a formation fraternity exist which is not deeply rooted in the contemplation of God in the world while being open to the poor and to the signs of the times (RegNB 9:3)? Can there be found a more stimulating pedagogical motivation for a formator than the following intuition of a famous contemporary mystic, "Those who are aware of their own wounds are the only ones capable of healing those of others?"

A further thought came to mind: In the formation of the brothers, can there be a greater joy than that experienced by three brothers, who during a desert experience had their cells ransacked by brother thieves who despoiled them of all their private goods while they were given over to the highest contemplation on Mount La Verna, where they were spending a few days? Can one imagine a more consoling experience than that of the rest of the brethren, who showed more than motherly care for the brothers who were robbed, joyfully dispossessing themselves of their superfluous goods in order to come to the aid of those who finally had experienced "perfect joy?" The experience of absolute nonviolence and the unsuspecting friendship of Brother Francis for the robbers of Monte Casale (Fior 26)—does that not invite present-day friars to walk the same paths? The search for peace with oneself and with others—could that not become a basic principle of the pastoral vocation? Peace, tolerance, and perseverance in working for peace—are not these simply so many fruits of the Spirit which could again launch the brothers on new apostolates?

All the novice masters received their grain of wheat in a spirit of willing cooperation and carried it back to their provinces as an invitation to be themselves converted to the Gospel and as a stimulus towards proposing to others a process of conversion in a convincing manner. They all proclaimed their willingness to obey, after the example of Francis, even a novice of one day (LM 6:4; LP 11), so that by an ever more evangelical and critical discernment they might come to a deeper knowledge of article 40 of the new General Constitutions: "Every friar is a gift of God to the fraternity. Therefore, even though they possess different characters, cultures, customs, talents, abilities and qualities, the friars are to accept one another just as they are and as equals so that the whole fraternity may become a privileged place of meeting with God." And all prayed in their mother tongue—including Tagalog, Urdu, Moba, Breton, Latin, and Malgache—to our Lord and to our Lady of the Angels so that the Spirit of the Lord might bring to fruition the promise of excellent fruit in the good soil of their lives in the bosom of the brotherhood (2Cel 109). In this way "their offspring will increase in numbers and in grace everywhere, and will extend its branches, wonderful for the abundance of fruit, even to the ends of the earth" (2Cel 23).

These insights constituted the fourth fruit of the meeting at Assisi, which the brothers attributed to the action of the Holy Spirit.

Soon after, the Masters returned to their fraternities and the friars of the general curia returned to the Eternal City. All gave thanks to God for everything they had seen and heard, as well as for all the gifts of the Spirit which the Lord had granted them with such magnanimity.

Rome, November 22, 1988

Chapter 3
1989-1990

1989

14. How some ministers of the Elder Daughter of the Church visited the Holy Land in the year of the bicentenary of the Great Revolution

Background: In February 1989 the author participated in a pilgrimage to the Holy Land with the ministers provincial of France. That year was the 200th anniversary of the start of the French Revolution. The following text revolves around these two themes.

In the year of the bicentenary of the Great Revolution, the second year of the Intifada in the state of Israel, the year of the ecumenical assemblies in Basel and Seoul, behold, a good number of ministers and servants of Gaul, plus Brother Samuel from the distant country of Vietnam, set out on a pilgrimage to the native land of our Lord. Their guides were a certain Brother José Luis from Spain, who had undertaken biblical studies in Paris and Jerusalem, and Brother Leopold, Commissary for the Holy Land in Paris. Also accompanying them was a certain Brother Transalpinus, definitor already for some years for the French-speaking countries of Europe, who deemed that a renewal of his energies at the very fountains of the Gospel was necessary for his work in Rome.

These ministers and servants wanted to follow closely the footsteps of Brother Francis, who in the sixth year of his conversion had decided to visit Syria in order to announce the Gospel to the Saracens (1Cel 55), but who, on account of many mishaps on land and sea, succeeded in arriving there some years later (1Cel 57). Our pilgrims, borne aloft on the wings of Brother Wind, landed in a matter of hours at the land sanctified by the life on earth of our Lord Jesus and his holy mother.

The friars wished to take very seriously their new General Constitutions which invited all the brothers to hold in great veneration the Holy Places (#122) and the prudent legislation which placed upon the ministers the ultimate responsibility for the ongoing missionary formation of all the friars, without forgetting their own (#137). So they were well disposed to accept the signs which the Lord would show them for the strengthening of their service to the brothers. They therefore passed some days profitably in fasting, prayer, and fervent meditation on the Scriptures. Their desire was not so much to see stones and venerable buildings, relics of the past, as to be transformed themselves into "spiritual stones" for rebuilding their fraternities. In that way they might better understand what the Spirit is saying to the brotherhood today.

Here then are some of the Gospel intuitions which lighted up their journey to the Orient, while they engaged in numerous readings of Scripture and meetings with brothers and sisters of all the Christian communities, with patriarchs and consuls, Jews and Palestinians, guardians of the Holy Places, and professors of Sacred Scripture or archaeology.

Liberty, the beloved daughter of the Great Revolution, they quickly realized, is a gift of God given to all people without distinction because, having come into the world with the Spirit of the Lord, it is destined for all without distinction. The Lord's entry into human history and the progress of the "evangelization of cultures," of which the General Constitutions now speak (#94)— have not these events caused the barriers of race, sex, language, wealth, and dehumanizing poverty to fall? Yet to this very day these barriers are opposed to the announcing of liberation in every continent and in the Land called Holy as well. Should not the brothers and sisters of Blessed Francis embrace peace first of all in their own hearts so as to be able to announce it forthwith, without prejudice, to all men and women of goodwill? Did not Brother Francis enjoin upon them, as their first task, to "desire to have the Spirit of the Lord at work within them" (RegB 10, 8)? As the Apostle Paul says: "Where the Spirit of the Lord is, there is freedom" (2Cor 3:17).

This then is the first grace which our pilgrims gleaned at the end of their pilgrimage: If they did not with a pure heart remain faithful to the contemplative dimension of their vocation (GC 29) and always open to the renewing Spirit of the Lord and his Good News of liberation, it would be impossible for them to animate their brotherhood and to fortify the faith of each friar. They themselves should first of all be free in order to set free (Gal 4:31). They would never be able to console, edify, exhort, or sanctify others if they did not first allow themselves to be wounded by the

Passion of our Lord Jesus and by the sufferings of the poor. Specifically, it was on Mount Tabor and in Jerusalem, where, in accordance with the vision of peace of Isaiah (Is 2:1-5), all the nations shall gather together, that they gave thanks to the Lord for this intuition.

With regard to the **equality** of all people and what it implies, the pilgrims were anxious to obtain an answer above all from the Scriptures and from Brother Francis. In this bicentenary of the Revolution, much had been said about equality and its importance in our multicultural society. Brother José Luis explained to them as best he could that in God there is no exception of persons (Rom 2:11; Eph 6:9; Gal 2:6), that before God Europeans and Orientals, Jews and Arabs, Christians and Muslims are brothers and sisters. God's own insertion in Bethlehem in the country of Judea and thus in human history with all its religions and cultures wiped out any superiority of one race over another. In this context our pilgrims recalled the fact that their brotherhood had again solemnly defined itself in the last Pentecost Chapter as a community of equals, whether clerics or laics, having the same dignity and even competency before God. So they prayed long in the desert of Judea and in Jericho, whose walls had been thrown down by the force of faith, that the Roman curia might allow itself to be convinced by the eloquent example of the life of the brothers and recognize the way of life of Brother Francis, according to whom all were equal in dignity, without distinction. In their provinces they had some years ago acted upon the happy intuition, originating in the Gospel, of abolishing all civil and even curial titles and in accordance with the command of the Lord, deciding not to call each other "Father," much less "Very Reverend Father," but simply "Brother." So they gave thanks to the Lord for this revolution in interpersonal relations in the name of the Gospel.

Every day and in every place the pilgrims from Europe experienced the call to search for **fraternity**, not from the sources of any human revolution but in the Gospel which has a wonderful transforming force. As never before they recognized with greater clarity that the manner of living of the brotherhood should be rooted in the "humility of God" (EpOrd) because God took on a human form in order to "enter into the situations of conflict inherent in human history," as one of them would later say. While they were sailing from Tiberias to Capernaum their meditation centered on fraternity. As another of them said: "Fraternity is like a fragile boat being battered by winds and high seas in the post-

revolutionary, post-modern, secularized context of our society."
With complete confidence in the Lord the brothers entertained the
hope that God would remain with them if they should prove
capable of being constant in prayer, as well as ready, intrepid, and
firm in their resolve to follow Jesus in today's world.

They became more and more convinced that the way of life of
St. Francis and his brotherhood would still attract people of all
times and ages, also in their country. And during this boat trip yet
another conviction took hold of them, namely, that it was necessary, first and foremost, to begin with the conversion of their own
hearts. Only then should they set about changing structures. This
was how the brotherhood could be faithful to its vocation and give
a witness of peace, of justice, and of respect for human rights
because all three values have their ultimate source in God, as had
been pointed out so clearly by Irenaeus of Lyon: "The glory of God is
the person fully alive."

At the close of this deep meditation one minister spontaneously
read a passage from the General Constitutions which illustrated
very well what the friars had been trying to live in their country
for quite some time. Suddenly it took on a greater clarity: "The
whole fraternity, that is, the Order, the province, the friary, as
well as every friar, is not to live for itself alone; it must benefit
others and seek that same fraternal fellowship with all people
which it cultivates in its own midst. . . . In order that the Church
may always be seen more and more as the sacrament of salvation
for our time, the friars are to set up fraternities in the midst of the
poor and in secularized groups and contexts. They shall consider
them a privileged means of evangelization" (87:1,3).

When at last they came down to Tabgha, the traditional site
of the multiplication of the loaves (Mt 14: Mk 6), they came to a
unanimous decision. They would celebrate upon their return to Gaul
a chapter of mats of all the provinces. Here they would meet all
the friars, share with them the bread of life and the bread of
faith, and hold a discussion on evangelization in "the global
context of the world and of our country," giving special attention to
the cooperation of all the provinces and all the friars. They
clearly understood that this dynamic development of their own
vocation and of their structures should, when God saw fit, be the
fruit of their self-evangelization. One of them expressed it in the
following words: "You can only evangelize what you love." Having
come to the end of their pilgrimage in the Holy Land, they
returned giving thanks to the Lord in the words of Psalm 150 for

having brought them thus far and for having opened up new paths for them. Indeed, their souls had experienced a wonderful renewal.

> Praise him [the Lord] with trumpet sound, praise him with lyre and harp! Praise him with tambourine and dance; praise him with strings and pipe! Praise him with clanging cymbals.

Then Brother Transalpinus gave the ministers a brief homily on their future commitments, taking as his inspiration the words of St. Augustine: "You are the trumpets, the psalters, the zithers, the tambourines, the choirs, the lutes, the flutes and the sonorous cymbals" (Exposition of the Psalms). With that each returned home.

Jerusalem, February 1989

15. How some friars of the West meditated on the wisdom of a proverb from the Far East which says, "When God closes a door, he opens a window" (China)

Background: In June 1989 H. Schalück together with R. Kellerhoff (Werl) and Th. Diederich (Hong Kong) undertook a journey of reconnaissance in the People's Republic of China. The journey took them, among other places, to Beijing, Jinan, Xi'an and Shanghai. It was the time immediately preceding the bloody repression of the students' movement.

Towards the end of the second last decade of the second Christian millennium, when everybody spoke of the evangelization of cultures, behold, some people looked out from the center which is in Rome, to recall the discovery of the West Indies by Christopher Columbus, an event to be solemnly celebrated in the year 1992. Others, on the contrary, particularly brothers and sisters from Africa, Asia, and the Americas, who in these latter centuries had discovered European missionaries in their countries and had endeavored to begin intercultural dialogue with them, looked rather towards the periphery—for them, towards Europe. They began to ask both themselves and the Europeans whether that continent, having now attained partial unification at the political and economic levels, might not finally discover its deeper spiritual and cultural roots.

Still others, animated by a no less holy zeal, were conscious of the fact that the year 1994 would mark the celebration of the seventh centenary of the arrival of the Friar Minor John of Monte Corvino in distant Beijing, where shortly afterwards he was appointed patriarch "of the entire Tartar kingdom." These friars withdrew their attention for a moment from the curia which is in Rome in order to direct it instead towards the East, towards that mysterious Celestial Empire, in an effort to understand better, with the grace of God, what the inhabitants, Christian or otherwise, of that vast country could say even now to their brothers and sisters in the rest of the world. The doors and seaports of that country had for long remained closed. In recent years, however, the words of that great wise man, Confucius, had begun to come alive. Two thousand years ago he had sung, "How happy I feel to be able to salute friends coming from so far!"

Three friars of the Province of Saxony in Germany had heard the words of this most friendly salutation from the very lips of other friars now living in China. And the names of those who had undertaken the journey to the East in the month of May in the Year of the Dragon were: Reinhart of Werl, Theobald from the island of Hong Kong, a man who had already proclaimed the Gospel in China before the great revolution, and a certain Transalpinus who for some time now had been residing in Rome.

It was during the novena of Pentecost, the time at which the Roman Church prays incessantly for the coming and help of the Spirit, that the three pilgrims crossed the Pearl River to enter Guangzhou (Canton). From there they made hurried visits by land, sea, and even on the wings of Brother Wind to the great cities of Xi'an, Beijing, Jinan, and Shanghai. Meanwhile they asked themselves what the Lord might help them to discover for the benefit of their own conversion. Always and everywhere the Saxon visitors manifested towards those brothers and sisters of the broad smiles who rushed to meet them on their bicycles the desire of Francis: "The Lord give you peace!" Day and night they endeavored to capture the meaning of those words welling up from the inexhaustible fount of Oriental wisdom, words they had read before their journey: "To understand the people you meet, you must concentrate much more on what they do not say and on what they are perhaps not able to say."

Whenever the brothers entered a house or met with people— events which were like genuine gifts to them—they thought of the proverbs of Lao Tze: "Whoever is able to see that which is little is clairvoyant. Whoever is always gentle is truly strong." Finally there occurred to them one of the rare words of the silent Buddha which they always recalled: "Patience is the best of all prayers."

So it happened that having been spiritually fortified in a thousand ways and interiorly strengthened, they spent the whole octave of Pentecost in the Celestial Empire. Even more—by a rare working of grace they came to perceive with greater clarity than ever the wonders which the Spirit of the Lord had accomplished during these latter years all over our sister and mother Earth.

"Be transformed by the renewal of your mind" (Rom 12:2).

In recent months in various parts of the earth, the call to a "new mode of thinking" had made itself heard—a call to hope, to singlemindedness, to the participation of all people in political systems and the various social structures. These transformations had their beginnings in the East but they have also had their repercussions in the West. Others emphasized that the Apostle Paul had been the first to speak of such a renewal so that this invitation was first of all directed towards the Church and to the preachers of the Gospel. Even in the city called holy and eternal, there was increased awareness of the fact that people are more important than any system, more important even than the sabbath (Mk 2).

In the Celestial Peace Square, where they happened to be on the vigil of Pentecost, but also in other great squares and in the streets, the three friars had the experience of meeting thousands of young people, men and women, who demanded that the leaders of the country adopt a new mode of thinking. They asked the visitors where they had come from and what thinking had impelled them to come from the periphery towards them, towards the Celestial Empire. The three Saxons spoke to them of their country of origin, of their Father and Brother, Francis, and of the meaning of the salutation of peace. They also gave witness, when they were asked (RegNB 16), of the hope which animated them (1Pt 3:15). They told them how Brother Francis would salute others as brothers and sisters, no matter what the color of their face, the form of their eye or nose; also how for the Apostle Paul it was not important whether one were a Jew or a Christian, a European or an Asiatic, a Chinese or a Saxon of Westphalia. Because of the Lord Jesus, all people were in the embrace of God's love and were called to enter his Kingdom of peace and justice. Some of the local people with whom they had engaged in long conversations left them these words of Tao as a departing message: "Heaven and earth are united and refreshing rain falls on the good and the wicked."

"Surely words like these," said the three travelers from the West, "allow us to discover traces of the Kingdom of God and of the incarnation of his Gospel where no one might have expected it." They also asked, "Would not a dialogue of religions and of cultures be necessary for the greater good of all and for the building of a world of peace and justice?" Yet again the friars asked themselves to what point the new thinking had been absorbed by the leaders and those wielding power in that country. A young woman gave them an answer by quoting Confucius: "Do you wish to know whether a country is well governed? Pay great attention to the music which evolves in that country."

And with a smile she continued: "Do you think that music is nothing more than the beating of drums and the sound of bells?" Amazed at the profundity and the accuracy of these observations, the three friars were dumbfounded while they recalled their own country and their cities of origin.

When they began to speak of nonviolence and the building up of peace on the model of the Gospel, an old man who had alighted from his bicycle quoted Tao: "Meekness overcomes force and violence. We must leave the fish in the deep waters. Offensive arms of the state should remain where nobody can see them." The three companions had nothing more to add.

Some days later, when they had already returned to Europe, they had with no little consternation heard the news that those in power had resorted to using arms against their own sons and daughters in Celestial Peace Square. They remembered the words which they had exchanged with their hosts in that same square. Their prayer then became twice as insistent, asking that as soon as possible peace and justice might again embrace each other (Ps 85:10) in that country. For "Nothing is more gentle than water, but nothing is stronger than water to wear down hardness. The defeat of today is a step on the way to the victory of tomorrow." And the three, always more eager for the wisdom of the Orient, gave thanks to the Lord for this consolation.

When the sun goes down in the West, it rises in the East.

In the great city of Jinan, capital of the province of Shandong where long ago friars from Germany, following the missionary example of their brother, John of Piano del Carpine (+1252), former custos of Saxony and minister provincial of Cologne, the three pilgrims stayed on for a longer period in order to meet the bishops, priests, and their brothers and sisters in the faith. They heard them speak of the "great ordeal" (Rv 7:14), of all kinds of persecutions and tribulations, of the many dangers that the Church had suffered in Asia (2Cor 1:8-11) and still suffered even to this day. However, the brothers also heard them speak about perseverance and fidelity. Recently the obstacles had become less and several churches had been reopened. The people who were walking in darkness began to see a great light (Is 9:1).

The friars were now able to visit the cities and towns of Shandong, where missionaries from distant Germany had scattered the seed of the Gospel. Here both the young and the old approached them and told them with tears in their eyes how they had withstood trials and how they had endeavored to construct a Church after a new model, one built of "living stones" (1Pt 2:5). They spoke of a Church which, according to the recent ecumenical council and with the approbation of the Lord Pope, would be at the same time Chinese and universal, Roman and catholic, giving and receiving, evangelizing itself and taking its place among sister Churches in other cultures.

With exceedingly great joy the three companions saw that there was only one Gospel, only one Church in the name of the Lord Jesus. They exhorted everyone to preserve this unity constantly and prayed more insistently to the Lord of History that the penetration of this new thinking should make itself felt everywhere, including Rome. They prayed, too, that the Lord Pope would soon be able to honor the Celestial Empire with one of his numerous visits. Furthermore they decided, as a preparation for that visit, to call the attention of the Roman curia to a saying of that most catholic man, Matteo Ricci (1552-1610), a member of the Society of Jesus, which for long competed with the Lesser Brothers in the evangelization of China: "We can hope that many of their ancestors have been saved because they obeyed the natural law and God, in his great goodness, came to their aid."

Since the friars were ignorant of the yin and the yang and were rather tied up in their neo-scholastic mode of thinking, a mode that was exclusive rather than inclusive, abstract rather than concrete, and since they yet had no idea of what message the Church and culture of China could bring to humankind and the Universal Church, they once more opened Tao and read: "An image speaks more than a thousand words. When the sun goes down in the West, it rises in the East."

When they asked a theologian of the country the meaning of the word *inculturation*, he told them this parable: "Some students held a lively discussion on this proverb of Lao Tze: 'He who speaks does not know; he who knows does not speak.' When the master came, they asked what the meaning might be. 'Which of you knows the perfume of the rose?' When they all said they knew, then the master said anew: 'Describe that perfume in words for me.' They all closed their lips silently."

The yin and the yang

Having come to the end of their journey, the three pilgrims took part in a festive meal in the house of the bishop along with other guests. At this meal the artistic presentation and order of the plates resembled the temple which is to be found in the Forbidden City and bears the name of "Celestial Harmony." In its reconciliation of contraries, this temple is an image of the harmony full of tension and the tension full of harmony which seems to impregnate and be diffused in the whole culture of the country. They were served softness and hardness, sweetness and bitterness, fluidity and solidity, the brackish and the piquant, the flesh of animals and the flesh of birds, the serpent and the dove, the frog and the fish, the raw and the cooked, the boiled and the roasted, the animal and the vegetable, the hot and the cold.

All this wonderful individuality and this universal complementarity had remained hidden from the three travelers until that day or had appeared to them worthy of detestation because according to their Western way of thinking these contradictions had appeared irreconcilable.

Strengthened in body and soul, enriched in an unforeseen manner with new experiences of faith, the three friars returned to their country of origin consoled in the very depths of their being by this fourfold conviction: (1) The seed of the Gospel and of the Kingdom of God produces varied fruits in a multiplicity of ways; (2) The Lord of History is the same yesterday, today, and tomorrow, but the world in which God's Kingdom is to come is rich in diversity; (3) There is a time for sowing and a time for reaping; a time for weeping and a time for laughter; (4) Where God closes a door he opens a window.

And the pilgrims said to one another that perhaps the moment had come in which the Lesser Brothers of different countries, all those who had once been expelled from China in sorrow and tears, could enter the country once again by a window, now in a state of deeper purification and of more profound conversion to the Gospel of the Lord of History.

Beijing, June 1989

1990

16. How Brother Francis preached in the ruins of the former Franciscan church in East Berlin

Background: The following text was written shortly after the fall of the Berlin wall. The occasion was the last East-West friars' meeting held in January 1990 (cf. the background to #6).

At the beginning of the year of our Lord 1990, as the human family had just begun a new decade and at the same time was beginning to prepare for the third millennium, as the peoples and the Christian Churches of Europe were asking themselves with special urgency how they could contribute in their old continent to the new thinking, behold, it came about that all of a sudden a great concourse of people came streaming together to gather in the pitiful ruins of the former friary of the Lesser Brothers in East Berlin. In fact, word had spread in wonderful fashion that in that place in which the friars from Brandenburg and Saxony had for many centuries lived in poverty to sing the praises of God, Brother Francis was to preach a sermon which would throw light upon the many dark and difficult questions posed by the recent turn of events. And there were also together about sixty of his brothers who had in those very same days hurried from East and West, North and South, even from the eternal and holy city of Rome, that they might meet together. With God's help they meant to read and interpret the signs of the times and in particular investigate the saving consequences of the so-called "perestroika" in their own brotherhood and ask themselves in all this what the Lord of History wanted of them in this momentous hour.

When a vast throng of people had gathered, tourists and natives, German-speakers and Slavs, Prussians and Bavarians,

Europeans and people from the two Americas, Christians and those of other faiths, Brother Francis lifted up his voice and said:

Blessed are those who have the great bravery of hope. One day they will know the meaning of the words: "The snare is broken and we have escaped" (Ps 124:7).

Blessed are those who carry no arms, who are open to dialogue and to mutual fraternal correction and who are meek. In them the nonviolence of our Lord Jesus celebrates his great coming.

Blessed are the contemplatives. In the struggle for peace, perseverance in the vision of God is like a net stretched beneath trapeze artists.

Blessed are all those who can think globally and act locally. In them the great utopia of the Reign of God is brought about in small steps.

Blessed are those who find words and gestures of encouragement, consolation, and active nonviolence in moments of need and persecution. In them Jesus will rise up in Lubljana, Prague, Dresden, and El Salvador, in Vietnam and Beijing, at the Nevada Test Site, in Bucharest and Rome, and anywhere on earth.

Blessed are the intrepid and the patient. They are like roses blooming in the desert. They are like a shepherd's sweet-sounding flute inviting heavy walls to dance in chorus.

Blessed are you when you know how to hear the voice of the people and to understand rightly their silence. You shall be the advocates of the poor, sisters and brothers in the new human family.

Blessed are the vulnerable. You shall be collaborators for a civilization of enduring peace.

Blessed are those who commit themselves to peace, justice, and safeguarding Creation through the witness of their lives, more with concrete attitudes than with words. They shall be a symbol of God, the friend of humanity.

Blessed are you when you know how to use creative and liberating utopias instead of legalisms and ideologies inimical to life and the human person. You shall be even more useful and will have much more to do.

And then Brother Francis added in his customary brevity of speech some words to explain what all this has to do with the Kingdom of God:

The Kingdom of God is like the tenderness and the strength of those men and women, wherever they are, who believe that Good is stronger than Evil and that Evil in history and in the individual will be overcome by Good. The Kingdom of God is like the endurance of these "hammerers at the wall" who never give up their hope for openness and liberation, who strive to look beyond where we are today.

The Kingdom of God is like the warm shelter and sweet-smelling soup kitchen in a remote corner of that Roman palace in which watch is kept over the purity of Catholic teaching. The Kingdom of God is like the mild glance of Mother Teresa of Calcutta, who begged to have this place. It is like the vision and large-heartedness of the Lord Pope who granted it to her.

The Kingdom of God is like the joy in faith and the political courage of the basic ecclesial communities on all continents and also in this city. For in them the word of God is spoken among the poor. In them liberation is achieved and celebrated in the Holy Eucharist.

The Kingdom of God shows itself in the fasting and prayer of those countless sisters and brothers who bear witness in the Nevada desert against the senseless overproduction of atomic weapons, against that poverty created by humans throughout the world and who stand for the life of the cosmos. They point out that the deserts of unrighteousness and destructiveness can become a garden full of good things.

The Kingdom of God is like the courage of all those brothers and sisters who have, like those in Romania, remained steadfast through decades of affliction and now see a great light.

When a young brother then interjected a question, asking which perspectives he could indicate for evangelization in the year 2000, Brother Francis answered in these words:

If you want to build a ship, do not begin by calling men together to gather wood, to prepare the tools, to distribute this and that task, to divide up the work. Rather set about arousing in them a longing for that wide, endless sea, which may be compared to God's liberating word for all people.

Thereafter Brother Francis disappeared again as quickly as he had come, and all returned to those places from which they had hurried here, some to the South and North, others to the East and West, and others again to Rome.

Pankow-Berlin, January 6, 1990

17. How the brotherhood was invited to reflect on the spirituality of the "Third Eye" and of "Pluridimensional Listening"

Background: The following text deals with the preparation for the General Chapter called to meet in San Diego in 1991. Its main topic was to be Evangelization. Beginning with the (fictitious) discovery of a manuscript of a writing by St. Francis, the text revolves around old and new approaches to a Franciscan view of mission and evangelization, not least around the Oriental idea of the "Third Eye."

During the last decades of the second millennium and in spite of all the progress made in science, technology, and theology; while the world witnessed the spending of 1.8 million dollars a minute on armaments; while 1,500 children died every hour from hunger or diseases caused by hunger; while every day the mortal danger of nuclear threat, of the destruction of the environment, of the contamination of the ecosystems, of the crisis of foreign debt increased, and the tension between the privileged North and the deprived South intensified, behold a certain Brother Miguel from the Basque country, the librarian of the Roman study center dedicated to St. Anthony, proceeded to index the numerous volumes and dusty manuscripts of his library. He would thus provide a database making the volumes more accessible to researchers, in accordance with the admonition of the Lord Pope to place the computer at the service of evangelization.

To his great surprise he came by chance upon a parchment largely devoured by "moth and rust" (Mt 6:19), which bore the mark of the Tau and the signature "Brother Francis." Before this document could be catalogued and confided to electronic memory, it was scientifically examined and analyzed by specialists from the whole world and from the brotherhood. Before continuing with this discussion and what resulted from it, let us say that both methodological limitations and Franciscan minority constrain us to admit that the results of the analysis are at the stage of a working hypothesis. If they should succeed in demonstrating its authenticity, this document would shed a new light on the mission of the whole brotherhood and on its missionary spirituality.

It appears that Brother Francis was an expert in the theology of the "third eye" and of "pluridimensional listening," of which the recent Chinese theologian, Choan-Seng Song (+1929) has been the first to speak to us. This vision of God and of the cosmos permits us specifically, as others have already confirmed, to capture the most profound dimensions of reality which can be hidden from the "carnal eye" (Adm 16) and to which Western theology, greatly influenced by the Angelic Doctor, did not have access until now. These dimensions very clearly show where it is possible to perceive "the seeds of the Word and the secret presence of God, both in the world as we know it and in other cultures and religions," about which our new General Constitutions so clearly speak (93:3). What follows will reveal in few and simple words what had been buried under the dust of centuries and what it would appear that the Spirit of the Lord wishes to make known to the provinces and the conferences of the Lesser Brothers.

To their astonishment the experts read: "A painter ought not to paint that which he sees before him but that which he sees within him." Did these words originate, as some people maintain, with the German painter, Caspar David Friedrich? There are others who do not wish to exclude the possibility that here is hidden an authentic intuition of Brother Francis, who had left to others the task of formulating it in this manner. Had he not, indeed, loved every human being, every brother and sister, Christians, Saracens and other unbelievers, the rich and the poor, Europeans and Americans, Thai, Méo, Khmer, Moi, Nung, Nhang, and Cham of Southeast Asia, as creatures of the same God who had placed the divine image in the heart of each individual? Do not all men and women, no matter what their color or creed, bear within themselves the seeds of the Kingdom to come? Had not Brother Francis, before preaching the objective truths, himself begun with his own conversion to our "God who is forever minor," the God of the Gospel? Had Francis not made obligatory a similar conversion for all his brothers and sisters? In this manner could he not come to be the example for all Franciscan evangelization, which in all cultures and in Rome as well should have as its starting point a "vital and fraternal dialogue" instead of stale disputes with words (RegB 3:10; RegNB 11:3)?

A young friar from Transylvania, responding generously to the call from the minister of that province, had volunteered to become a new missionary to the Celestial Empire and had made a study of the language. To the amazement of all he succeeded in deciphering some Chinese characters on the parchment which said: "The meek person is more powerful than the strong." Later the manuscript read: "The thickness of your sandals is of no use to you. The hardness of your fists is unavailing. The rapidity of your speech or your pen counts for little." Having read and listened to these words, all began to ask what meaning they were intended to convey.

A more detailed study of the document, this time on the part of specialists in patrology, led to a passage of the Protrepticon of Clement of Alexandria:

> The Word said to man: For me you are a flute, a temple. . . .
> The Lord has blown into a beautiful instrument, into man,
> that is, because he has made him in his image. He is the
> instrument most finely attuned to the divinity, to
> supernatural wisdom, to the heavenly Logos.

The document also yielded a statement of St. Ignatius of Antioch, one finally retrieved from the caves of oblivion:

> Become absorbed in the melody of God. Together you will
> all form a choir and thanks to your concord and harmonious
> love the song of Jesus Christ will be raised. That is the song
> which the Father hears; he will then recognize you as
> those who belong to Christ.

A certain Brother Theofried, professor of theology in Mainz and member of the theological commission of the brotherhood, added to these two texts a parallel one from Basil the Great: "When dogma is accompanied by a harmonious melody we embrace the words more readily, thanks to the pleasure which we experience on hearing them."

All were amazed at the perspectives which all these thoughts could open up for Franciscan evangelization now and in the future. Did not Francis himself, while speaking of God, use words such as "beautiful" and "melodious" (Praises of the Most High God)? Had he not taught his brothers to evangelize themselves and others with sensibility and solidarity while getting to know both the ancient and modern melodies of all cultures? Would it not be necessary that alongside the Gregorian chants there should also resound in the choir of the Roman curia and its imposing corridors other melodies, reminding one of the African proverb: "A sweet melody puts the worst demons to flight"? Could we not realize the possibility of living the truth of the one Gospel and the mystery of the one God with tolerance and in minority in every culture (GC 100), in that way uniting the most diverse voices and instruments in one magnificent symphony, respecting the diverse cadences which give rhythm to the history of God with us and availing of the flutes and cymbals which sometimes appear strange, exotic or even strident—all for the beauty of the ensemble? Did not the theology of Hans Urs von Balthasar, highly regarded in Rome, say that truth is "symphonic"? And had not Brother Ludovicus, on one of his reconnaissance journeys into China, brought the message: "Faith is like the song of a bird when the night is still dark"? Likewise Brother Gwenole from Gaul, president of the commission for dialogue with Islam, was fond of quoting a mystical passage from that religion: "Do not despise the man you see dressed in tatters, for beneath those rags may be hiding a great maestro."

The working groups charged with the preparation of the theme "Evangelization 2000" for the next Pentecost Chapter made an inventory of what they were able to learn from the discovery made in the Via Merulana and from the "Theology of the Third Eye" so as to include it in their pre-chapter working document.

Finally, it was also possible to decipher a mysterious refrain which, according to results of research carried out by the Africa Desk in the general curia, could have come from the natural religion of the Kple of Ghana. It was certainly known to our Brother Francis of Assisi and could cause the Gospel priority of care for creation, one which the friars had already promised to uphold, shine with a new splendor. The refrain says:

> Oh man, my brother, you hold in your hand the power over Earth, our Motherland. Raise up your eyes to the Lord above, and thank the Giver for all his love. The bird who drinks water looks up to say "Thanks" and gives glory to God in the highest.

A certain Brother Bernard from India who worked as assistant treasurer in the general curia found a refrain similar to a saying of a wise man of his country, Rabindranath Tagore: "God is not pleased with the great kingdoms but cherishes all the littlest flowers."

A certain Brother Francis from Mexico, who was an expert in the evangelization of the Americas, was convinced that he discerned a lament which, if it did not come from Francis himself, must surely have come from the high plateau of Peru: "Once upon a time people wondered at the Earth and wept for joy; now the Earth wonders at people and weeps for despair."

Had not Brother Francis heard in all of creation, even mute and silent creation, the voice and the melody of God, and had Francis not therefore venerated and protected it? So the friars decided in holy obedience to contribute by deed and word so that a saving rainbow might wrap all creation in her mantle; so that creation would be protected with care and healed where ravished; so that the rights of people and of creation would be deemed more valuable than economic imperatives; so that "universalism" rather than "eurocentrism" would in future be the desired goal. They became more aware than ever before that the harm they had done to others and to creation was first of all inflicted upon themselves. By the example of the little Brother Francis, they learned that effective ecology has its origin in a pure and peace-loving heart (Adm 16) and that today's utopias and dreams of a new heaven can tomorrow transform our earth. Indeed, "The power of the weak is found in the weakness of the strong" (Vaclav Havel).

When the brothers recognized what treasures had been hidden beneath the dust, they resolved to give a new future to their past, to walk as lesser ones, step by step, towards the great utopia of the Kingdom of God, to review the reality of the world with the "Third Eye," in accordance with the modulations of "Pluri-dimensional Listening," applying good as a remedy for evil, light as a remedy for darkness, while marvelling at the harmony of opposites in the universe and having utter confidence in the action of the Spirit of the Lord.

A certain Brother Arnulf, a well-known missiologist from the Netherlands, was given the commission of preparing a congress on the following theme, "Whoever beholds the sky in the water can see fish swimming on the trees." In distant Chile a certain Brother Ramón Angel of Chillán thereupon set about composing a cantata, which would in due course be played by the Sweet Flutes Ensemble in San Diego, on the occasion of the Pentecost Chapter, taking his inspiration from the words of Martin Luther King, Jr., "I have a dream...."

Rome, June 13, 1990

18. How a friar from Europe spent the time of Lenten penance in Indochina

Background: During Lent 1990 the author received an official entry visa for a visit to the friars in the People's Republic of Vietnam. This enabled him to remain for five weeks in that country. As far as is known, this was the first extended visit of a foreign religious after the revolution of 1975.

"Where there is no prophecy, the people cast off restraint" (Prv 29:18)

Shortly after Ash Wednesday of the year of our Lord 1990, a few weeks after the beginning of the Chinese New Year placed under the sign of the horse, many realities were dissolving because many a dream had more strength and vitality than they. Frontiers began to be turned into bridges. In Prague a former Catholic "dissident" ruled as president of the new republic and was greeted as a friend by the Lord Pope. In East Berlin a Protestant pacifist, who up to a short time before had undergone much persecution at the hands of those in power, was named Minister for Disarmament. The worldwide meeting of the Christian Churches on justice, peace, and respect for creation in Seoul cast a hopeful glance at "Noah's Ark 2000"; and the Franciscan family was at long last an NGO [nongovernmental organization] at the UN. The cause of the Doctor Subtilis from Duns in Scotland was being examined with favor in the Roman Curia, and the Order of Lesser Brothers, with a view to the coming Pentecost Chapter, began to occupy itself with "Franciscan Evangelization in All Cultures."

While these things were taking place, behold a Germanic brother working in the Order's curia in Rome read in Hermann Hesse, a poet from his land, this sentence: "For the possible to happen, the impossible must be incessantly attempted." For he had been struck, aside from all the important affairs, files, and decrees, by the words of the biblical Book of Proverbs which had been read out in his Curia at the beginning of the time of penance and which declares: "Where there is no prophecy the people cast off restraint" (29:18). Others meditated on the words of the famous Leonardo da Vinci, who said: "The end of one thing is the beginning of another." All the brothers wanted in those days to understand better what the Spirit was saying to the provinces and fraternities in the whole world and to the Roman Curia so that they could prepare themselves in obedience to the Lord Pope for a new evangelization in all the cultures of the globe.

And so this brother, who was otherwise often to be seen in Rome, applied himself once more after many unsuccessful attempts to obtain from the authorities of that mysterious country in Indochina which today bears the name "Socialist Republic of Vietnam" the necessary travel papers for a visit to the brethren there. He wanted at long last to see with his own eyes what the Lord of History had revealed to the brothers of that province in the fifteen years since their liberation. As those in power saw that he did not cease to ask, and after they had assured themselves of the purity of his motives, they allowed him into their country and gave him everywhere a sure guide.

And so, with not a few difficulties, he spent almost the whole time of Lenten penance in Vietnam. He hurried through the land from the Mekong Delta up to the frontiers of the Middle Kingdom. He visited all the fraternities, listened to everything that each one had to say to him, greeted some of the bishops, ate with them, and could not refuse all the many invitations of the men and women who concern themselves with the temporal prosperity of that land.

And what he experienced during those weeks of pre-Easter pilgrimage, he has recounted in a few words for his own benefit but also for the benefit of his curia and the whole brotherhood.

"The brothers shall not make anything their own and shall not dispute with others over anything"(RegNB 7:13)

The brothers in that tropical strip of land lived after their "Liberation" in the indestructible spirit of perfect joy which is the sure sign of a true evangelical vocation, in the spirit of God's preferential option for the poor. Those in power had taken away from them as from the whole Church many privileges and many big houses and other properties. For example, in the former seraphic college in Thu Duc a farming cooperative is today growing mushrooms, and in the former large clericate in Nha Trang the Communist Party is today spreading its atheistic teaching and training its cadres. So it was that the brothers, driven out of the center, learned to know the richness of the poor periphery. And that which appeared to them bitter in this—namely to have to live without property and without letters of protection—was revealed to them ever more clearly with God's help as the way of conversion to the Gospel for the Church and for the brotherhood. Indeed, they accepted it more and more as "sweetness for body and soul" (Test). For they realized more clearly than ever before that the Lord of History wanted to purify and evangelize them more radically through extensive suffering (Rv 7:14) so that they might become better heralds of the liberating message of Jesus Christ and render an important service to the whole brotherhood, wherever it might be.

Preaching more by their lives than by their words, the brothers were courteous and helpful towards everyone, the powerful and the atheists, but also the Buddhists, animists, and those of other faiths, as befits the lesser ones. They sought in everyone the image of the living God, collaborating with all for the good of the people and for the good of the poor, insofar as this was not against their conscience or their Rule. And to everyone everywhere they said the words of greeting of their little brother Francis of Assisi: "The Lord give you peace." So in those years the brothers possessed nothing apart from their humble places and a few hens, pigs, and dogs. They preserved the bond of their brotherhood, which held them together and strengthened them. In all things they had an unwavering confidence in the Lord, who spreads in all cultures the seeds of divine, indestructible love and thereby lives and rises again in all forms of society, even in the so-called "new" ones, especially in those where it is most unexpected.

"And the brothers should work" (RegNB 5; RegB 7)

Another important aspect of the Franciscan calling—namely work with one's own hands—so our pilgrim reported, was also rediscovered by the brothers of that country in the socio-political conditions of the "new society" with God's help as a grace. The Mighty Ones after the "Liberation" of their country laid upon all citizens in strict obedience the duty of carrying on some honorable work. On those who did not know how to or did not want to they imposed the duty of learning some skill in order to avoid idleness and, as they expressed it, "to contribute to the building up of the nation." And the brothers discovered thereby, even though not without much anguish and much pain, that they are members of an organism which suffers and to whose healing they have to contribute, that they must above all be in solidarity with the poor. They learned in many ways a new manner to be "minores" and thereby to be "subject to all who are in the same house" (RegNB 7:1), living from the work of their own hands just as Brother Francis had wished it long ago (Test). And so some brothers had begun to plant rice, pepper, bananas, and many other sorts of fruits and vegetables and to work every day in the fields. Others kept water buffalo, goats, sheep, and useful fowl. The whole fraternity in Suoi Thong, not far from Dalat, had developed to a high degree of perfection the art of breeding silkworms. Others again worked in the sweat of their brow in factories and cooperatives. Still others visited and healed lepers, both by means of human contact and of modern medicines. Yet others cured with local herbs and tinctures many other human sicknesses—yes and even the sick cattle.

Since those in power saw that the brothers served the people in everything, they came to trust them more and more, allowing them increasingly to break for the poor the bread of God's word and of the Eucharist. And the bread and the wine which the brothers chose to use for this had the bitter taste of the earth and the sweet scent of those who, precisely in contradiction and conflict, are the sacramental signs of a radical immersion in the mystery of the God who heals the world through his own wounds (1Pt 2:24). And so by the sweat of their brows, in the praise of God and the celebration of the active and creative memory of their liberation, did the brothers give witness to the presence of such a God. In everything they lived out the Lord's commission, to give people bread instead of stones, fish instead of serpents, eggs instead of scorpions, peace instead of discord, love instead of hate, always overcoming evil with good. They still witness today to the fact—and this applies to all forms of society wherever they may be—that human life is more than work, production, and consumption. The brothers give witness to the deeper values of life, to which God has called all men and women—love, friendship, respect, capacity to share, solidarity. And in everything they are signs of the emptying of Jesus and of the Church, which has been sent to all cultures in all times, to serve and not to rule (Mt 20:28).

". . . and persevere in doing what is good" (RegNB 21:6)

Through the brothers in Vietnam and through the example of their evangelical life in the midst of a society in conflict—and this is the happy result of this troublesome pilgrimage—many brothers elsewhere, wherever they are, can acquire new insights into the mission of the evangelization of cultures which the Lord has given to them. For these Vietnamese brothers were esteemed to be worthy of bearing many a pain and persecution in order that the whole brotherhood, interiorly cleansed and purified, might in every age and in all cultures and continents bear a more credible witness to the hope which lives in it. And it is this which the brothers in that land would like to say to all the other brothers and sisters today:

-that there is a time for sowing and a time for reaping; a time for speaking and a time for remaining silent; a time for dying and a time for new life, which, however, always comes from the hand of God and can be a fruitful seedbed of the Gospel;

-that this is the fasting which the Lord desires (Is 58:6-7): not to bear arms, either in reality or in thought, to seek the seeds of good in everyone, to live an active nonviolence, to bring about reconciliation, to bring together in unity what is divided, to share with others hope and bread, to heal wounds and to cultivate a sense for the long-term perspectives of the Kingdom of God;

-that whenever he takes away, the Lord also gives; for example, new, unexpected impulses for a life in accordance with the liberating Gospel and, not least, numerous new brothers also;

-that the Kingdom of God is already begun wherever people seek and celebrate freedom; where dreams of a new life open horizons and overcome systems of human making; where peoples, tribes, and religions declare peace with one another and begin to build together a common tent.

And our pilgrim returned shortly before the solemnity of the Ascension of the Lord to Rome and to his curia, tired out and covered with the yellow dust of that land yet interiorly cleansed and more deeply converted to the Gospel than was possible for him before.

Ho-Chi-Minh-Ville (Saigon), April 1990

19. An open letter to the winged creatures of the world; today's
Franciscan preaching to the birds

*Background: Legend says that Francis of Assisi preached to the
birds. The following paraphrase adopts the form of an open letter.
The author is fully aware of the liberties he is taking with the
original and the danger incurred in so desiring to interpret this
famous text. In any case, this letter is addressed not so much to the
birds as to all those committed to the future of our Churches.*

To my beautifully feathered brothers and sisters on this day,
October 4, of the year of the Lord 1990, the feast of St. Francis
    In the year 1979 the Lord Pope John Paul II declared our little
Brother of Assisi patron of ecology because the Poverello discerned
in every creature an image of God and was the first who desired to
preach not only to men and women but also to the birds and the
fishes. On the occasion of the XXIII Day of Prayer for World Peace
(1990), our Holy Father has again called Francis by this title.
    I now desire to send you an open letter so as not to lose contact
with you. And first, I beseech all the diligent carrier pigeons
among you who experience an increase in your work, though not in
your wages, to please hold me excused.
    Here are some reflections and questions which you may study
during your meetings and upcoming synods.

A Bird's-eye View

You have not failed to observe that, in spite of the evolution of
humanity towards a global village, the horizons of our brothers
and sisters within our Churches have on not a few occasions become
restricted. The human species and its material needs occupy the
stage, especially in our ancient Europe which desires to change its
plumage. Many are they who think only of themselves, forgetting
the wider perspectives of solidarity. If we do not succeed in seeing
beyond our noses or further than the rim of our nest, Europe will
very likely be transformed into a fortress rather than into a house
of many rooms. It will be the poor here and elsewhere who will
suffer, as well as our living space. Many brothers and sisters
engaged in politics and commerce and also some brothers and sisters
in our Christian Churches have thus far exploited and exhausted
our Mother Earth and its vital living space. They seem to forget
that in God's plan the flowers and herbs, the air and water, fish

and birds, and the ozone layer are our brothers and sisters. We should therefore treat all creation with attention and respect, love and compassion.

In our Church even though many from among us have had very positive experiences in contact with other cultures and other theologies, these people have sometimes been branded "exotic birds" or "rare species." They could, however, have so much to contribute to the thought and faith of Europe. I am convinced that there will be many more people who will understand the need for thinking globally so that they may take action locally. You are an inspiration for them.

For all those of you who stop off in Rome while on a new journey to Africa or to the Middle East, I hope your stay will be a happy one, full of enriching experiences and that you will have a safe journey home.

Never Cease to Learn

Dear brothers and sisters, feathered friends of the world, what most of all attracts my attention is your capacity to grasp the "new thinking." It is now several years since some migratory birds had observed signs of this new thinking among politicians close to Moscow. I am pleasantly surprised to see that you form one family in which the humble sparrows and the simple swallows, the larks and the hummingbirds, the owls and the kakapos all enjoy for the sake of the common good the same dignity as the peacocks, the robins, and the cardinal birds with their fire-red plumage.

Unfortunately, humans continue to insult one another with names such as "fat bird," "old magpie," "goose," and other such nicknames. It pains me when your names are discredited in this manner and I wish to ask your pardon for this attitude of my brothers and sisters, as well as for that "right of first picking" which they have so egoistically invented, thus projecting their thirst for power and their hatred upon you.

It would be so beneficial to learn from you. On our way towards the third millennium we are in dire need of becoming conscious of the dignity of all people and religions, of the need for sharing what is the patrimony of all, of the need for fraternal solidarity among all, of God's preferential option for the wounded birds of all times and of all places, of the necessity to build a just and peaceful world for all.

It is high time that we give you thanks for your good example, also for the way in which you deal with your refuse—so ecological, intelligent, and nontoxic—and ensure its recycling. Was not our Lord Jesus the first to speak clearly in praise of your creativity, of your happy gift of combining very creatively short-term improvisation with long-range visioning and planning? In short, did he not speak in praise of your excellent sense of priorities (Mt 6:25)?

A New Solidarity—Even Among Humans?

Faced with the problems which more and more trouble humanity and also our Church, we ought to open our eyes more widely, broaden our horizons, and listen to each other. To adopt the policy of the ostrich, sticking one's head in the sand to avoid seeing problems—is that another projection by my fellow humans on you? Such a policy does not solve anything.

Some years ago our brothers, the German bishops, in a letter dealing with the ecological crisis, raised the alarm: "The human race is filling its vital space and that of many generations to come with the refuse it produces and consumes. It is causing the destruction of elements on which our life and growth depend." They went on to affirm that humans can protect themselves from the destiny they themselves are preparing only by recovering their solidarity with all creation. Otherwise they will become slaves of a creation which they so proudly aspired to dominate. What beautiful words for the evangelization of our modern world and of our hearts! But, who is going to pay attention to them if not you, our dear winged creatures? Thank you for your inspiring example.

Another specific element on which the life of our world depends is likewise endangered—the capacity to listen to the melody of others, the capacity to dialogue, the faith, not in one's own power, but also in the things God wants to tell us through other people and religions. God gives us so many signs of the liberating power of the Gospel, inviting us all to live it in ever new ways.

You, birds of the sky, fly peaceably on the breath of Brother Wind. You remind us of the Spirit which blows where it wills and which can renew us and carry us afar. Pope Paul VI in his letter *Evangelii Nuntiandi* has called to mind that those who announce the Gospel must first of all be evangelized and inwardly converted themselves. And his successor, Pope John Paul II, has highlighted that need during his numerous journeys on the wings of Brother

Wind, on devout pilgrimage to so many cultures, religions, and especially to the poor.

A Final Greeting

In conclusion, my dear brothers and sisters, the birds, I should like to invite you to renew your confidence in humanity and use the possibilities offered by so many churches and other ecclesiastical buildings so as to build your nests and face the winter. Numerous facades, restored at great cost, are now ready to offer you a dwelling at low rent, not to mention the many empty rooms available in some of our institutions which could give you lodging. We have so much need of your intuitions in our institutions! Let us console ourselves mutually and meditate together upon a saying of Rabindranath Tagore: "God becomes tired of mighty kingdoms but never of a little bird."

October 4, 1990

20. On the manner in which the brothers, gathered at the Portiuncula, jointly wrote the *Ratio Formationis Franciscanae* (Plan for Franciscan Formation)

Background: A gathering in Assisi of brothers responsible for post-novitiate formation around the whole world had before it in October 1990 the draft of a new formation plan for the whole Order.

In the year of grace and freedom 1990, the year in which the brothers of two provinces of Brazil began to celebrate the centenary of the arrival of missionaries from Saxony in Germany and in which one of them sent its first missionaries to Angola; the year in which several frontiers disappeared, never again to be instruments of separation between people of goodwill but rather to unite them and enable them to share in a common destiny; while the brotherhood prepared for the Pentecost Chapter under the protection of Blessed Diego of Alcalá; following the commemoration of the transitus of Francis, our Father and Brother, behold, about one hundred and twenty friars, all of them masters and formators, gathered under divine inspiration, each with his letter of obedience from the general curia in Rome. This meeting in the Portiuncula was for the purpose of studying the priorities of

Franciscan formation and of drawing up a document that would be important for the whole brotherhood and for the world. This document they decided to call a "Formation Plan" or *Ratio Formationis.*

During the four weeks of their stay at the Domus Pacis, their sharing of ideas in an atmosphere of peace enabled them to gain a profound understanding of what the Holy Spirit is saying today to the provinces and to the brothers. Following an inductive rather than a deductive method, they were full of joy at the sight of the many signs of life and growth which became obvious throughout the brotherhood. To all of this they gave expression in the *Ratio* we have mentioned, intended as a means of helping the friars to enliven and cultivate all the gifts of the Spirit which may lie dormant in them, namely, the gifts of contemplation and of action, the gifts of the word and of silence, of animation and of organization, of teaching and of study, of preaching and of working with their hands, of caring and of consoling.

Some of the results of that meeting are set down here in simple words for the edification of all those sent by God who may desire to improve their formation and to instruct their brothers.

First of all, they dedicated themselves to contemplation in all its aspects, under the guidance of a certain Brother Premanand of Bengal. The name of this dear brother means "The Beloved of God." To introduce us into the mystery of education in the Spirit of God and to make us become conscious of the grandeur, the beauty, plus the difficulties of educating young friars, he utilized particularly the profundity and the mysterious complexity of art, especially the art of music. He began by quoting John Chrysostom, Doctor of the Church, and spoke to us, using his words: "There is no greater art than that of education. The person to whom this art has been given must be a more complete artist than a composer, a painter, a sculptor or a musician."

Granted what he called the dynamic character of Franciscan formation and education, he quoted a mystic of his own country, distant India: "Does not the sorrow of unsung songs break the strings of my lute?" (R. Tagore). Finally he quoted an anonymous German poet who, upon seeing the walls of Europe collapsing, had exclaimed: "When the Lord intones the ode of history, I want to be flute, guitar, harp and cymbal. I would wish him to inspire me with sweet music and melody."

Brother Premanand earnestly exhorted all to come to know and learn new songs, new rhythms (Ps 96:1)—the music of wind and sea, the unfinished symphony of the universe, the hymn of flowers and the murmur of rocks, the melody of a pure heart and the steady chant of the other cultures of religions, particularly those of the poor; to remember also—if it should be necessary—that after the example of certain figures who have preceded us in the faith, it is possible to sing in a furnace (Dan 3) as also in the belly of a whale (Jon).

Thanks to these suggestions, all those present reflected on the best way to proceed in future in the formation of oneself and of others.

Next came the discourse on holy theology. A certain Brother Anthony, a most learned man coming from a university situated in the holy city called Eternal Rome, gave an exposition on theology as a science according to St. Bonaventure of Bagnoregio and Blessed John Duns Scotus. After this all shared their own experiences and reflected on what they should say in the *Ratio* about this sacred science. They recognized more clearly than ever how important it is for the Lesser Brothers to interpret at once courageously and humbly, in the power of the Holy Spirit, the signs of the times both past and present (GC 4) and to conceive liberating utopias for the future. They should remember that it is a matter of general experience that those without utopias or dreams become transformed into slaves and are filled with hatred.

They came to understand that for all people there is a propitious time—a time for meetings, articles, and scientific symposia, but also a time for attending the school of the poor and working in a soup kitchen (G. Gutierrez). Was it not true that the Lord had explained his word to our Father Francis when, through the inductive method, he led Francis among the poor in order to show mercy to them (Test)? So from now on, the younger friars, wherever they may be, should understand more clearly and, with eyes and hearts illumined, announce as "minors" the good news of the "God who is forever minor." This means that with a watchful eye and in solidarity with the suffering Christ in the heart of today's world, we should look more carefully into the face of the poor. It was not necessary, Brother Anthony confirmed, to look for anything else in the living heritage that our illustrious predecessors Bonaventure, Duns Scotus, and others have left us.

And they all reflected on how to proceed better in the future, in the formation of themselves and others, thanks to these suggestions.

Then the important treatise on history was taken up. A certain Brother Francis of the empire of the Aztecs and the Mayas gave notable exposition on the subject, "Whoever has no memory has no history." He declared that in the brotherhood as well as in the universal Church, it was important to write and to understand history, not as a history of victors and conquerors, but as a history seen from the perspective of the humble, of the oppressed, and of all those who had been outcasts from their countries, those who, according to the promises of our Lord, will one day possess the land (Mt 5:5). He knew how to stress in a gentle but convincing manner that for those of us who have promised to become genuine minors, the history of evangelization should not be written nor taught with the eyes and hearts of those who commanded the ships of the *conquistadores*. It should rather be perceived through the eyes and the anguished hearts of those who in previous centuries were standing on the seashore and looking out at the ships of the approaching conquerors. In this respect he advised us to structure the study of history, of our faith, of our Church, and of our brotherhood in such a way that it could be of interest to all marginalized brothers and sisters of all the continents who are nameless with no one to console them and have even been forgotten by official history.

All began to reflect on how to make better progress in renewing themselves and others, thanks to these suggestions.

The brothers gathered together in the Portiuncula did not neglect to reflect upon a new pedagogy and a new psychology which could be very useful at least for the internal growth of the brotherhood. A certain Brother Hyacinth of South Africa gave a learned discourse on the theme, "The road is open ahead of you but the obstacles on the way are within you." With great sensitivity he showed how the friar who is called "master" and formator must himself be constantly learning; how we as "minors" can learn from the poor; how active nonviolence is a virtue not of the weak but rather of the strong and courageous, of those who are pure of heart (Mt 5:8). He showed how important it is to accept the dark shadows in one's life, to transform one's anger into strength, to have the patience and the bravery to advance by slow steps, never looking down upon the small and insignificant. He exhorted all in the words of the famous Thomas More not to abandon ship because the wind is so much stronger than we are (Utopia), but rather to learn thoroughly and patiently the strength of helplessness. He ended his words by saying: "If many little people in many little places of the world do very many little things with a little bit of courage, something great can happen." When they heard this they realized that in the new *Ratio* reference should be made to love for the "dimly burning wick" (Is 42:3) and the glance full of love for the "bruised reed" (Is 42:3). For even in this age of computers and satellites, the most effective techniques of communication continue to be attentive listening, fraternal conversation, and fraternal correction. So all the brothers, wherever they may be, should be convinced that the only constant in their life is the need for continual conversion.

Again all the friars reflected on the best method of making further progress in their own formation and that of others, thanks to these suggestions.

A short but important chapter was devoted to asceticism. Brother Nicholas of North America spoke about the hurt that can come from the struggle against the unjust suffering of the humble and the poor and about the commitment not to capitalism or socialism but to a more just order for all people. He complained vehemently that in the brotherhood there are still ministers and brothers for whom one of the most dangerous sounds in the world was that of brave, committed people who thought in a loud voice. He said it was a question of sharing with compassion in the passion of Jesus in the poor of today. He wished all brothers, wherever they may be, to recognize more clearly that "Those who suffer enrich and heal the world." He demanded that the friars, both clerical and lay, exercise without distinctions and with equal dignity and competence the ministry of reconciliation, of peace, and of solidarity with the weak. He urged them in the spirit of the Poor Man of Assisi to regard that which they found repugnant as a grace.

Again they all realized that something should be inserted in the *Ratio* concerning this renewed asceticism.

Finally he developed the theme of evangelization and the third priority of these six years—formation in a missionary spirit. In the "Preliminary and Marginal Notes" of his presentation on this theme, a certain Germanicus of Freiburg stated that a fraternity which is not a serving fraternity is of no practical use. The Church of Jesus, he said, should at all times, including our times, valiantly bear the memory of Jesus by being in the front line of the struggle in favor of the utopia of the Reign of God, of peace and justice and the reconciliation of humanity with the entire cosmos. There is question, he said, of sowing in many places, in the spirit of creative fidelity and of faithful creativity, the gospel seed of hope in the future and being able to wait patiently for growth and the harvest. Something which should not be one of the lesser preoccupations of the brotherhood is being a sign of salvation among men and women even under new forms (GC 84; 87:3).

The brother called attention to the necessity of studying other languages and of establishing numerous international fraternities as witnesses of the new world and new forms of evangelization. For it matters little—and this was his final word—that a brother come from Bavaria or Bengal, France or Guinea, Thailand or Germany, Saxony or Singapore since all are equal in Jesus Christ (Gal 3:28). He exhorted each member of the fraternity to undertake a new Exodus, using the words of a Buddhist proverb: "The frog that lives in a fountain has no idea of the immensity of the ocean." Therefore all must learn to see further than their noses in order to recognize with new and pure eyes the traces of the Reign of God in the entire world and in all of creation.

All the brothers took to reflecting on what they should do in order to be formed themselves and to form others, thanks to these suggestions.

By way of ending this memorable reunion, the brothers held a silent prayer meeting around the little chapel of the Portiuncula, in that very place where Brother Francis had been "formed" by the Lord. Having spent one hour in silent contemplation, all heard, each in his own language, the words which Brother Francis spoke from high up on the ancient walls:

If you wish to provide for one year, sow some grain.

If you wish to provide for two, plant a tree.

If you wish to provide for a hundred years, consecrate yourself to your brothers. Because if you sow grain, you can only harvest once.

If you plant a tree, you will be able to harvest ten times. But if you form human beings, you will harvest a hundred times."

He then added in a low voice:

"You have one teacher, and you are all students" (Mt 23:8).

Then they all went home consoled and strengthened, filled with salutary restlessness—the formators to their provinces and the others to Rome, to the place called the curia.

Assisi, November 1, 1990

Chapter 4
1991-1992

1991

21. "And God saw"—The story of a new creation

Background: One account in the Book of Genesis describes God's creation of the world in six days. Each day ends with the verse, "And God saw that it was good." With deep gratitude to the biblical writer, the author has adapted that format in an effort to describe how humans could move toward the unity which God built into creation at the beginning.

And God saw how human beings throughout the earth, from East and West, from North and South, without distinction of race, religion, or sex began to weave close bonds of friendship. Nations chose their best men and women and sent them to that famous glass palace on the island of Manhattan, which is open to all the nations on the earth. There they began to listen to one another, to learn from each other's history, to understand each other, and to elaborate common projects.

And God said: "It is good that it be so." And this was the first day of a new era.

And God saw how peacekeeping soldiers separated armies of the nations still at war; how disagreements were healed by prudence and negotiations rather than by arms; how the leaders of the nations began to listen to the voice of their people and how all jointly began to prefer the good of the whole universe and the peace of a united world over private and national interests.

And God said: "It is good that it be so." And this was the second day of the new planet.

And God saw how human beings began to love and protect creation rather than exploit it—the air and the ozone layer, water in rivers and oceans, the earth and all that lives and germinates. And God also saw that human beings no longer dominated or exploited one another but, recognizing themselves as children of one Father, treated each other as equals.

And God said: "It is good that it be so." And this was the third day of the era of new thinking.

And God saw how human beings throughout the earth began to search out and eliminate the causes of hunger, sickness, ignorance, suffering and debasing poverty; how they began to share in common that which belongs to all; how in view of the common good and of life at world level, they began to see the positive aspects and the points of convergence of all races and religions.

And God said: "It is good that it be so." And this was the fourth day of the new creation.

And God saw how with an admirable sense of responsibility and without the thirst for power, human beings began to utilize the natural resources which had been entrusted to them, particularly combustible material taken from the earth and atomic energy; how their conscience was always alert and prompted them to consider whether all the new projects were in accordance with the service of God and of humanity and especially of the poor; how they abandoned arrogance for sensitivity, greed for unselfishness, egoistic individualism and nationalism for the spirit of a new and lasting solidarity.

And God said: "It is good that it be so." And that was the fifth day of a more human world.

And God saw how human beings on all the continents set about dismantling and destroying their rocket launching pads, their arsenals of bombs and munitions, their chemical and biological weapons of destruction as well as their spy satellites and detection systems; how they disbanded their armies and, consequently, initiated in all their schools and education systems a pedagogy of peace so evident and logical that conflicts could be solved by peaceful means.

And God said: "It is good that it be so." And it was the sixth day of a new heaven.

And God saw how human beings finally began to recognize him as the God in love with life; how they considered the struggle for peace, justice, and the integrity of our wounded creation a true worship of the living God; how each time that one of their ideologies failed, when proposing a new constitution they would write: "Let us never lose sight of the one God, who is the beginning and the center of a just and human world. And as human beings, alive and free, peaceful and without arms, let us be signs of God's healing presence in history."

And God said: "Now all is well." It was the seventh day of the creation of the universe which, for the future, belonged completely both to a new humanity and to the one God of all peoples.

February 1, 1991

22. How certain brothers recognized the truth of the words: "The Lord reproves the one he loves" (Prv 3:12)

Background: In March 1991 the author accompanied Minister General John Vaughn for the last time. This journey led once more to Eastern Europe, through Hungary to Transylvania (Romania). The text attempts to portray aspects of the new beginning after the period of Communism.

In 1991 at the beginning of the month of Ramadan, as Christians were starting their penitential season before Easter—during the week in which Desert Storm in Arabia and Mesopotamia began to abate, lo! Brothers John of America, William of Britain, and Transalpine Hermann, all belonging to that house in Rome called the curia of the Lesser Brothers, set out for the East. They traveled to the regions once known by the names of Carpathia, Valaquia, Moldavia, Transylvania, and Dacia, regions now inhabited by the tribes of the Magyars and the Czechs as well as by descendants of people from Saxony and Suevia in Germany. The three pilgrims from Rome were anxious to visit their brothers living in these regions because for many long, dark years these friars had suffered a great deal of injustice and persecution. In these latter months, however, at the end of most severe affliction, the brothers now saw, in accordance with the plan of a benevolent God, a new light appear, and they began to awaken to new life. The pilgrims wished to experience, in the example of their brothers in exile, a new driving force for their own faith and the service they were rendering in Rome. They, on their part, came to offer these brothers encouragement and solidarity.

The three companions from Rome chose for their first stopping-place the country of the Magyars, a place called Szeged in the Province of St. John Capistran. Precisely here, on the banks of the river Theiss, is located the ancient friary where Blessed James of the Marches had been guardian. On their arrival the three companions were greeted by Brother Claudius, the minister of that province, and by the local bishop. During the previous forty years, those with power in the land and those who had embraced an ideology opposed to God had profaned this building and had all but destroyed it completely. In these latter years, however, it was coming to life again in an extraordinary way. Our pilgrims were overjoyed to hear that under divine inspiration many young people were asking to be received to obedience as members of the three provinces of the Magyar tongue. In this same house, which was being reconstructed with great sacrifice and the contributions of numerous brothers the world over, these men would receive formation in accordance with the Gospel and instruction in sacred theology.

Brother John celebrated the holy liturgy, joined by all the friars and the people of the place; and its principal theme was "Whoever has not the courage to dream, does not have the strength to strive." In the name of Jesus they recalled the Exodus from Egypt and the crossing of the desert. For themselves and for all the oppressed, wherever they might be, they celebrated the memorial of their liberation by the Lord. And they asked the Lord of History to heal this dissolute world and to render their brothers capable, wherever they might be, of being servants of evangelization, of healing, and of liberation, now most of all when the Pentecost Chapter was imminent. Afterwards they renewed their strength with a good, strong fish soup and slept for some hours on hard straw mattresses. The three companions then set out once more under the maternal protection of Brother Claudius of Budapest, who had now become their guardian on this journey.

In Transylvania, which today forms part of Romania, they first visited the place called Maria Radna, where the memory of the Mother of the Risen Lord is kept alive. There, three very old friars, who had survived a long period of oppression, were overjoyed and immensely grateful for the visit. Other friars came from all the surrounding countryside as soon as they heard about the arrival of their guests from Rome. After having been forbidden to do so for so many years, they now took their habits out from their hiding places and put them on as a sign of belonging to a brotherhood which extends all over the world. This was also an act of thanksgiving for the fact that the Lord and their brothers in the whole world had not abandoned them in their time of exile.

When they had exchanged greetings and the kiss of peace and had fortified themselves with the large loaves and the dry wine of those cold regions, they went in procession into the sanctuary to thank the Lord and his Holy Mother for these signs of consolation.

When a huge crowd had gathered together from all the surrounding villages, they all sang this chant which, in a wonderful manner, the Lord himself inspired them to do at that moment:

Hail Mary, you who take upon yourself the hopes of the oppressed, sign of salvation and of unexpected liberation, you have been chosen by the Lord of History. Blessed are you among all the poor, because they see the fruit of your womb, their Liberation.

Holy Mary, Mother of Europe, of Latin America, and of all the poor in all the world and throughout all time, pray for us that we may listen to the Spirit of God and obey him in this hour in which the peoples of the whole world are becoming awake. May the hour soon come in which everybody may experience full and complete justice joined to a lasting peace; and where the new era of liberty may be there for all to see.

They then visited Temesvar, Deva, Hunedoara, and finally a place founded by the Germans, which bears the name of Hermannstadt. For that reason it held particular interest for Brother Transalpinus. After a tiring journey along the course of the river Moros and through the Carpathian mountains covered with snow, they reached Ciksomlyo in the Czech region, where the friars of the Province of King St. Stephen, (969-1038), even to this day care for the sanctuary of the Mother of the Afflicted. Here one can also see a slab which records that in August of 1938 the Minister General from Rome, a certain Brother Leonard Mary, had visited this sanctuary and the friars who take care of it. The three Roman visitors remained there for some days during which time they contributed to the heating of the bare cells by hauling great trunks of firewood from the woods, which were still under snow from the Carpathians. They held a meeting with the friars of the whole region and mutually updated their information about the death and resurrection of the brotherhood throughout Europe and other areas, giving thanks to the Lord for having changed bitterness into sweetness of soul and body. At the end Brother John celebrated the Holy Eucharist with the friars and all the people who had come in from the countryside.

And with great astonishment they heard the words which declare that the future belongs to the poor of all the earth, that the afflicted will be consoled and that the persecuted shall all receive a new home close to God (Mt. 5:l2).

They drank from the living font of the memory of a God who liberates; they ate of the bread which constitutes the sacrament of the closeness, the fidelity, and the solidarity of that God with this world groaning in birth pangs. As a salutation of peace and farewell and in the name of the friars of the whole world, they sang the Magnificat there facing the image of the Mother of the Afflicted: "The Lord himself puts down the mighty from their thrones and raises up the little ones" (Lk 1:52).

While our pilgrims were making the return journey from Budapest on the Danube to Rome on the Tiber, lo and behold, a warm spring sun shone over all the country. After a long and severe winter, the ice began to melt before the warmth of the sun, a fresh stream of water ran alongside the road, and in the clear air the first flowers began joyfully to adorn the plains and valleys of the Balkans. So the three companions returned to their curia invigorated, strengthened, and interiorly enlightened. Tired were they from their journey but deeply convinced that the Lord corrects, chastises, and purifies them and the whole brotherhood while simultaneously never ceasing to love them and build them up.

Budapest, March 25, 1991

23. How the brothers held their Pentecost Chapter in California

Background: *The regular General Chapter of the Order of Friars Minor took place in June 1991 in San Diego. In it the author ("Transalpinus") was elected as Minister General.*

Shortly after the feast of Pentecost 1991, about one hundred and fifty ministers, servants, and delegates of the worldwide brotherhood arrived in California on the shores of the Pacific Ocean to hold a chapter in accordance with the prescriptions of their Father and Brother Francis. They chose the city which bears the name of St. Diego of Alcalà (1400-1463). This is where the first friar missionaries, led by Junipero Serra, had begun the evangelization of this region and of its inhabitants. The friars, faithful to their origins but also open to the signs of the times, full of gratitude and with a pure heart, wished to reflect on the five hundred years of evangelization in the two Americas and to begin a new stage in the propagation of the Gospel in all cultures. After having listened in the first week to various reports and after having recounted to one another the signs of the growth of the kingdom of peace and justice, but also of the thorns and the thistles (Gn 3:18) of this difficult kingdom of earth (Mt 13), they were tired. Following the example of their Father and Brother, they sought consolation and inspiration from simple and exotic beings in the Balboa Park Zoo and at the famous "Sea World" of San Diego's Mission Bay.

Some admired the intelligence of the dolphins and the docility of the whales, which move forward very rapidly and in this are also an example for the ongoing formation of the friars. Others, especially those who are concerned with finance and new forms of fund-raising, lingered before the kangaroos who can make great leaps with their pockets empty; or else they contemplated the many-colored birds of heaven, who do not sow but reap just the same (Mt 6:26). Still others stopped fraternally near the lions, for according to the word of our Brother Francis (2Cel 194), the brothers who draw their knowledge and their missionary vocation from poverty and the contemplation of the divine mysteries are comparable to a "raging lion attacking everything with ardor." And did not the Lord Pope in his letter to the chapter solemnly reaffirm the bond between poverty, contemplation, applied study, and mission? Other friars strolled by some simple doves and cunning serpents (Mt 10:16) and by the falcons who once wakened Brother Francis, inviting him to profound prayer (2Cel 168).

After these visits all the brothers, invigorated and filled with new ideas, returned to their cells, to their coetus (language) groups, and to the auditorium which the Lord Bishop of the place had put at their disposal.

The day of the feast of St. Antony, under the presidency of a cardinal of the Roman Church, a new minister and servant of the whole brotherhood was elected. The lot fell on a brother who until then had been at the curia of the brothers in Rome as a Transalpine, but had also visited many times beyond Rome and Italy. He was so astonished and disconcerted that he asked in all confidence to be reassured and counseled by the Lord Cardinal to know what all this signified. The latter, full of goodness, took him by the hand and spoke to him this word of Oriental wisdom: "Every long and difficult journey begins with a first small step" and the words of Scripture: "The Spirit helps us in our weakness" (Rom 8:26), "The Lord disciplines those whom he loves" (Heb 12:6), and much will be forgiven to those who give proof of much love (Lk 7:47). Thereupon the brother minister, full of confidence, took the oath of loyalty and hope, promising to love everyone and to obey all the brothers. He also abandoned the name *Transalpinus* and took henceforth the name *Hermannus Universalis*.

After that the assembled brothers continued the *camino real* (royal road) of their own evangelization in the Pentecost Chapter, following in the footsteps of the great exemplary figures of centuries past. They decided upon a plan for the next six years, to bring the Gospel of our Lord Jesus Christ, under old and new forms, into the deserts and into the towns, into the centers and into the peripheries, even to the frontiers of the visible Church, for the building of the Kingdom of peace, justice, and respect for all created things and for all living beings. They recognized how much the example of Diego was for them precious and timely, a simple Lesser Brother, a superior, a missionary, a preacher, and a lay brother, who with great modesty and competence lived and preached the Gospel, not only in Spain and in the Canary Islands, but also in Rome at a time when the plague was ravaging there.

In their very special loyalty towards the Holy See, the friars solemnly promised to reorganize their formation and their study programs in the spirit of the Lord Pope and of his paternal letter and even to draw up a *Ratio Studiorum*. Here theology would have a choice place as a "practical and wisdom-bringing science," as a service of the poor and of their liberation, as a "speculation of a poor man in the desert"—just as the Seraphic Doctor had already said in his *Itinerarium Mentis in Deum*. The brothers recognized the great value of music for the following of Christ and the formation of all the brothers and sisters of St. Francis—a question not of training soloists so much as members of a world orchestra, who listen to one another, each in his own way and in obedience to a conductor, making his contribution to the harmony of the whole. Did not a most famous Swiss theologian, Hans Urs von Balthsar, write that truth is like a symphony? And are not human singing and playing before God, as Johann Sebastian Bach said, "our smile before God"? Will not the brotherhood in the future need many more musicians, dancers and storytellers in order to live and to spread his Gospel under new forms?

Towards the end of the Pentecost Chapter, the Minister of the whole fraternity went with two other brothers to spend forty hours in the Nevada desert, to pray and to give encouragement to the brothers and sisters who bear witness there in favor of a culture of life and peace and against a culture of war and modern arms. The brothers Ludovicus Vitalis and Alanus Gallicus, as well as certain sisters, informed them about this form of Franciscan evangelization. A certain sister Rosemary was astonished that the General Minister made his first pilgrimage to the desert and its surroundings and to some renowned sanctuary. And at the common celebration of the word and of the bread, a brother of the Quaker community wished the Minister the peace of contemplation and even of sleep in his service in Rome and beyond, like that of Jesus in the midst of the storm on the lake (Mk 4).

After their return to San Diego, the brothers saw a happy ending to the Pentecost Chapter. The Minister exhorted them all to set out on their homeward way with a new heart and a new spirit (Ez 11) and with eyes purified, in the certainty that a brotherhood which does not serve others does not serve any purpose, and that a people without vision is on the way to ruin (Prv 29:18). Finally, he sent his brothers back into their provinces and their fraternities, and he himself returned to the holy and eternal city of Rome, to the curia of the Lesser Brothers.

Rome, July 15, 1991

24. How the Minister of the brotherhood began his service in Rome

Background: The text describes some of the meetings and experiences of the new Minister General during the first months of his service—during his return to the "novitiate" in Rome and Italy.

After the Minister of the whole brotherhood had returned from the Pacific to the Mediterranean coast, shortly before the feast of the Blessed Bonaventure, he hurried to visit the Roman curia of the Lord Pope and some of the prelates in it so that in the name of all the brothers he could bring them the greeting of peace and promise, reverence and collaboration for the good of the Church and the Kingdom of God. At the same time he asked that together with his councillors and secretaries he might be admitted into the presence of the Lord Pope himself as soon as he came back from one of his numerous missionary journeys. Then in the curia of the Lesser Brothers on the Gelsomino Hill in Rome, the Minister began his novitiate, understanding better and by small steps the true nature of the commission which the Lord had given him through the Pentecost Chapter.

To begin with, he asked all the brothers who had remained on the Gelsomino during the Chapter their counsel about how he could best perform his service for the good of the brotherhood and who else could help him in this. Above all things they desired to live faithfully in accordance with the Rule and the Constitutions and to have a guardian, Thus, a certain Brother Aloysius, who previously had been at the shepherds' field in Bethlehem and had initiated pilgrims and young brothers into the mystery of the Incarnation, was named guardian. There followed several other brothers from a variety of provinces.

The new general council met together for several weeks, despite the great summer heat and dryness of Latium, in order to make a beginning of drawing up their own Six-Year Plan. These brothers tried to perform their manifold task with great creativity as well as sober foresight. On a particularly hot day the Minister encouraged them all with these words: "Let us plan with great foresight, like Noah, who began his building work before it began to rain." And they spoke of how important it was, on the occasion of the 500th anniversary of evangelization in the Americas, to understand the ideals of the young and the tears of the poor. In opposition to the inflation of words and the culture of noise, they affirmed the importance of living out a culture of stillness, contemplation, and listening and developing an ability to understand the secret message of music and of the other arts, even if it was only the message of the wooden violin of our Father and Brother. They wished to invite all the brothers to compose new melodies, rhythms, and dances

On the feast of the Portiuncula, the Minister of the brotherhood hurried to make his first visit as Minister (second only to a simple visit to the bare desert of Nevada) to Assisi in Umbria. There in front of the little chapel, he preached penance to the people who had hurried to gather from all points of the compass and at the same time he proclaimed the forgiveness and liberation which comes from God alone. He spoke of how the poor and crucified Jesus was for Francis the center of the Church and of how today the Lord Jesus is to be found in our impoverished and crucified fellow human beings. The important thing is to fight with a reconciled heart for the Kingdom of God, faithful to the commission of the Lord to Brother Francis to build up the house of faith, of fraternity, of the Church, and of creation. He reminded them of the inheritance which comes to us from the past. At the same time he spoke with no less urgency of the obligations which come to us from the future and quoted the words of a great and wise man from the East: "Indifference and lack of interest towards the poor are the primary forms of violence" (Gandhi). But he also quoted a theologian with a more Western orientation, according to whom the important thing is not to give alms but rather to bring about justice. Then he joined with them all to beseech the Lord for his brotherhood, that it might prove capable of casting out from its own ranks and communities not only the demons who are dumb but also those who talk too much so that all may preach more by deeds than by words.

On the evening of that same day there gathered in front of the Portiuncula a large crowd of young people, some two thousand of them from all of Italy and some neighboring countries as well. They had been traveling on foot to Assisi for a whole week in order to pray for the Spirit of the Lord, the spirit of pilgrimage, and the spirit of prophecy for their own lives and for the Church's journey and to obtain the Minister General's blessing. Standing on a wooden podium, the latter gave a brief account of the Pentecost Chapter and recounted how Diego of Alcalà, that blessed brother who had not received Holy Orders, was able to "inspire afresh a world grown old and tired" (Bull of Canonization). The Minister praised the young people for the example of their pilgrimage, given also to his brothers, "many of whom want to return to nature though few of them want to do it on foot." And then he spoke of the hope he cherished, that one day he might be able to send many of them on their way to Vladivostok, Novosibirsk, Almaty, to Albania and Samoa, Easter Island and Fiji, to Xian and Jinan in distant China. Yes, it might become necessary to send a new mission of brothers even to Germany, as in the times of Brother Francis. For, and here the Minister cited a saying from distant Rwanda: "What moves the heart will also set in motion the feet." Thereupon he imparted to them all a blessing. And a young man from Umbria, for whom a certain Brother John from that province begged a special blessing from the General Minister, thus strengthened, immediately began his period of probation in the friary at Monteluco, where he still is today.

A short time thereafter and long before the first rainfalls of autumn, the Minister undertook a few short journeys to prepare himself better for service to the whole Order. First, he went to a Chapter of Mats at San Severino in the Marches. In this place a great poet and songwriter had once become a member of the Order as Brother Pacificus (LM 4). In this place, too, Brother Francis had once seen a little white sheep in the midst of a great many goats and gently compared it to the Lord Jesus among the Scribes and

Pharisees. The Poor Clares of San Severino had later taken that sheep into their care and from its wool made a warm habit for him (1Cel 77-78). Now it happened that in San Severino the Minister noticed that he had forgotten his capuche. A certain Brother Aurelius lent him another because he had two; since then he holds the one worn by the Minister in great veneration. It was at this Chapter of Mats that the Minister announced his intention of calling together in the near future a meeting of all the brothers who are poets, singers, painters, sculptors, tightrope-walkers, and artists of any kind. All of them, he said, should help the brotherhood to recognize, with eyes and hearts purified, the mission, at once old and ever new, which flows from contemplating and listening.

On the way home they called on the Poor Clares so that together with them they might be mindful of the living heritage which Francis and Clare left to the Church. The Sisters made a promise to the Minister, who is today's successor of St. Francis, that they would make him a habit with a capuche. And as he traveled back home to his curia on the Gelsomino, the Brother Minister prayed fervently that he with all his councillors and secretaries might be made worthy of carrying out their service in such a manner that its truth would shine forth increasingly not only as a hard diamond but also as a tender blossom and a gentle accord. And the Lord Pope received the Minister and the general council sooner than they could have expected, imparting on them and on all that they had resolved to do his fatherly blessing.

Rome, October 19, 1991

25. How the Minister of this brotherhood made a visit to San Damiano and upon Mount Subasio

Background: This text originated in the autumn of 1991, during a stay of several days in Assisi.

After spending some months in Rome, the Minister decided to visit San Damiano once more. He felt a greater need than ever to return to the origins of Franciscan life, to the living example of St. Clare and St. Francis, in order to receive there new impulses for the mission of the brotherhood in all cultures today. Following the mind of Brother Francis (LP 106), he sought counsel even of the youngest novices, asking them in what manner our past may have a future and which signs of the times the brotherhood ought to follow with particular attention. In all this his plan was to beg the Lord to enlighten him creatively and in a salutary manner, to comfort him in the time of his own novitiate in the service of the whole brotherhood.

In that place which Brother Francis had built up with stones and in which he himself had become a living stone in the history of God's relations with the human family (1Cel 8) and which even today serves the formation of new brothers, he read in the *Capita practica ad Anatolium* of the Church Father Evagrius Ponticus a passage about the noonday devil, the vice of acedia. The brothers had complained to one another in the Pentecost Chapter that even today this is for many friars an obstacle on the way of the following of Jesus Christ, of ongoing formation, and of the new evangelization. This is what he read:

> The demon of acedia, who is also called the noonday devil, is the most pernicious of all. He attacks the brother at the fourth hour [10:00 a.m.] and lays siege to him until the eighth [2:00 p.m.]. First, he makes the sun seem to move only with great labor or not at all and makes the day seem to last for 50 hours. Then he prompts him continually to look out of the window and jump out of his cell to see if the sun is still far from the ninth hour [3:00 p.m.] and look around to see whether perhaps another brother might not be coming. Then the devil implants in him an aversion for the place in which he lives or against his whole way of life or against manual labor. He goes on to suggest that all love among the brothers has vanished and that there is no one left to comfort him. The demon depicts life as going on for a long time and makes present to him the burdens of asceticism.

The Minister reflected at length on these words. He also read in the Legend of St. Clare how at the time the Poor Ladies lived in San Damiano "there was no place for acedia because idleness was cast out by their burning fervor in prayer and in service of the Lord" (CL 20). He thanked the Lord for always having shown to the brothers in moments of stagnation and crisis the way forward by means of contemplation, poverty, and solidarity with the poor (SC 55).

The Minister of all the brothers therefore resolved to summon soon to the Portiuncula all those brothers who in each province are responsible for ongoing formation in order to confirm the entire brotherhood in fidelity to its origins and to the signs of the times, and to win back that missionary dynamism which always flows from contemplation and poverty. This meeting would be placed under the motto: "The only constant thing in the life of the Lesser Brothers is that they must be constantly changed and converted to the Gospel of Jesus."

3. Looking from the garden of St. Clare at the wide Umbrian valley and especially at the Portiuncula, our pilgrim became aware that, as the Pentecost Chapter had likewise repeated with emphasis, the brotherhood is called to new forms of evangelization. The brothers must learn to know and to love the thousand flowers which God makes blossom and bloom in the garden of his world. These are the signs of his Spirit and his Kingdom in the various cultures, continents, and religions, in the history of peoples as in the hearts of the poor, which must become more and more the protagonists of their own liberation, sacraments and signs of Christ, as well as prophets of the Kingdom to come. He had an intuition that the secret of the brotherhood's inner and outward growth lies in its capacity for sharing, in its courage to listen, and at times also to speak a prophetic word.

The new *Ratio Evangelisationis* for the whole brotherhood, which the Pentecost Chapter had likewise requested, would have to speak of the internationality of the brotherhood and of its mission. With no little surprise, the Minister read that this was how it was even in the beginning. In the mission to Germany brothers coming from several nations were sent out from the Portiuncula. They came from Umbria, Tuscany, Lombardy, from Teutonia, Swabia, and Hungary—twelve clerics and thirteen laics (Giano 19). Back in 1224 at the time of Pope Honorius, England was an international project with four clerics and five laics, who included Englishmen plus Italians, Lombards, Frenchmen, and even a diversity of brothers from the Transalpine regions (Eccleston's Chronicle 4).

So the Minister decided to send brothers in the near future in the same spirit to Uzbekistan, to Armenia, to St. Petersburg and to Moscow, to Scutari in Albania, to Burkina Faso as well as to Mongolia. And he understood ever more clearly that the brothers would have to learn languages as a sign of the universality of salvation, and not only the better known ones but also Quechua and Urdu, Bavarian and Hindi, Chinese and Arabic as a sign that God's loving kindness is already present in all cultures. It matters not

from what race or tribe one comes but rather that one should be able
to see God's image in every man and woman, each being able to meet
the other with sentiments of peace, as "minores."

And when noon came, the Minister slowly climbed up Mount
Subasio to do penance and to pray in solitude. In the presence of the
Lord he remembered all the brothers and sisters who bear in their
hearts concern for creation as their contribution to the life of the
world (Jn 14). On the heights of the Carceri, where the shrubs
become ever barer, he read part of Elizabaeth Barrett Browning's
poem "Aurora Leigh":

> The earth is full of heavenly signs,
>   and many a bush aflame with God's spirit.
> But only one who can see with his heart
>   removes his shoes.
> How many sit around
>   and look in the bushes
>   for nothing more than a few berries.

Is not all of creation, the Minister asked himself in that hour,
like a colorful garden or like a musical score with a multitude of
known and unknown melodies and harmonies, all inspired by the
Spirit of God? Do not those who pollute and destroy the earth
destroy themselves? And he perceived more clearly than ever
before that the earth can become for us only what we are for it. For
only those who protect and love the earth protect themselves and
build their own future.

When he had reached the top of the mountain, the Minister
rested awhile in front of an old, gnarled oak, which seemed to him
like a symbol at once of the groaning of creation and of the music of
the universe. And he prayed in the simplicity of his heart, not so
much for himself as for the whole brotherhood on its way toward
the third millennium, this prayer which the Spirit suggested to
him in that hour:

> Most High, Almighty, Good God,
>   let our life be like a tree.
> Give us roots that reach deep into the earth.
> Let us grow into a robust trunk
>   which stands erect in its rightful place.
> When storms rage, may it not fall
>   even though it should sway.
> May its leaves, after every winter, turn green again

as a sign that you give a hope and a future
to everything created,
as also to our brotherhood in all the world.
And in due time, let us bear those fruits
your Spirit alone can produce:
a conversion forwards, respect for one another,
peace in our hearts, the impatience of the young
and the wisdom of the old, humor, creativity,
patience with ourselves and with others,
knowledge of our limitations, trust in the Spirit of God,
present even in our world of today.

Then the Minister of the brotherhood returned from San Damiano and from Mount Subasio to Rome, to the place called the curia on the modest Gelsomino hill.

San Damiano, November 1, 1991

1992

26. Letter of Blessed Francis to all the peoples of Europe and to their leaders on World Peace Day 1992

Background: Francis of Assisi once wrote a letter to the rulers of the people. In a similar style the modern-day author addresses both the proposed opening up of borders in Europe and the fifth centenary of the evangelization of the Americas; the latter event has important lessons for the former one.

Brothers and Sisters,

To all of you: men, women, and children, to the young and the old, the Christians, non-Christians and atheists, to politicians and deputies, to citizens, clerics, and laypeople, I send these words from Chichicastenango in Guatemala: May the Lord grant you peace!

For some time now, I have been present in this Amerindian continent with numerous brothers and sisters in order to give thanks to the Lord for the historic changes which result from his action in and through the people. The Amerindians, in common with all the poor of all times, teach us what it means to hope and to wait and how we could together make preparations for the centenary of 1992.

The Lord in whom I place my confidence and to whom we all must render an account reveals to us the profound meaning of history through simple, peaceful, and apparently powerless people. The deeply felt conviction of being born free will never die in the hearts of men and women. From this place I plead with my old continent, with all its inhabitants and those in positions of trust: Abandon every kind of triumphalist policy and in 1992 choose instead a penitential celebration. In the collective memory of all Amerindians there is engraved the remembrance of having discovered invaders in their native land five hundred years ago. But their thirst for freedom is as inextinguishable as their brotherly and peaceful disposition to help Europe to free itself from the burden of its own history.

I, a poor little man and your brother, who have heard the cry of so many people, beseech you: "What thing does the Lord require of you but to do justice and to love kindness and to walk humbly with your God" (Mi 6:8)? Do not speak with haughtiness of the first, the second, and the third world. Are you not aware that only one world exists, only one history of humanity, only one Earth, which is the mother of us all? Do you not understand that all people live in mutual interdependence and are all dependent on one God; that they have a common destiny; that all have to give and to receive at the same time? No nation, no continent ought to enrich itself any more at the expense of the others.

Europe, no longer export your arrogance, your egoism, your conflicts, your arms, your poison, your manner of living and thinking. Rather believe in the creative and peaceful forces of those whom you have herded together on the margins of society, those, indeed, in whom the Spirit of the Lord is equally at work. Be mindful to pay a just price for the raw materials and the sweat of the laborers from the South. I am also mindful of the words of my brother, Bishop Oscar R. Madariage from Honduras: "Drugs are the only product of our countries which is paid well." Why not export to us more true forms of solidarity, respect, and help, forms that will allow us to be autonomous? Please stop sending us a civilization of consumerism and greed, built upon force and exploitation. Why not send us a civilization of fraternity, of respect and love for people? Give your first priority to ecology, to the protection of creation for its own sake in an economy geared to preserving life for the whole world. Ecologists should no longer be compelled to denounce poisoned products; producers should put on the market only what is safe, useful, and beneficial.

Europe, please give up talking about "development" according to your standards. Talk rather about liberation from all "oppressive, sinful structures," beginning with your own and the ones you have imposed on others. Our Lord Pope has often spoken about this need of liberation for the entire human family.

Peoples and governments of Europe, when you become converted and are disposed to pay attention to the poor wherever they are, you will be contributing to your own liberation and will be preparing your own future. Let yourselves be "contaminated" by the hope of your younger sister in the faith. In spite of all your progress, you have too often given to the world the image of people who have no hope left but have come to fear the worst. When you cease to hope, then what you fear begins to happen.

Let us together have a look at another event of 1992 about which the whole world is speaking. You want to establish the foundations of that which Brother Mikhail of Moscow calls the "European house," a project which the Lord Pope also has approved and blessed. Therefore I appeal to the politicians and the bankers: Don't make a fortress out of Europe. Make it rather a house of friends, with many apartments rich in color. Let the foundation you lay be respect for life. Let the walls be your search for peace and your respect for all cultures and faiths. Finally, let the roof be a tolerance like that of God, who sends rain upon the just and the unjust (Mt 5:45) and who reserves to himself the judgment of history. Let your doors remain open wide. Demilitarize your hearts and your arsenals. Set up in your continent institutions which allow a large vital space for the intuitions of people, for dignity and liberty and human rights.

Remember, you leaders of the people, that you have received a mandate from them and that for the time being your special duty is the liberation and the well-being of your fellow citizens. The people themselves are the subject of their future. That is why they desire to change their leaders every so often. Do not act as if you were able to change the people according to your whim. Never treat your people as the mere object of your politics. "Prepare the way for the people" (Is 62:10). Let justice be your daily bread and for the future let national security be called respect for rights and liberty.

And you, peoples of Europe, as peace-loving, kindly, brave peacemakers, in these latter times you have seen a great light. You have become brothers and sisters to all those who struggle for liberation and dignity. Your bravery and your deep intuitions have caused frontiers to become porous, have caused walls to collapse and flowers of hope to spring up. The "renewing of your minds," about which the Apostle of the Gentiles has already spoken (Rom 12:2), will not fail to open a way for you. You have experienced suffering and persecution. Many of you were not afraid to be precursors, "sowers," even martyrs. Your dreams and your utopias have achieved more than all the "Realpolitik" of so many politicians.

No one has ever succeeded in walling in those sisters of our faith, namely, liberty and creativity. You have shown to millions of your brothers and sisters throughout the world that to live in hope is worthwhile because the hopes rooted in the heart of a people produce more fruits than any ideology. Yes, you have demonstrated that the hope of the poor is long-lived and cannot be quenched. No regime or nation should in the future try to dominate or overcome another; nor should anybody again lay claim to a monopoly of the truth, apart from God. For that reason the various religions should not regard each other with suspicion; rather should they discover and recognize their common responsibility for the life of the world and the whole cosmos.

Your courage has served as a lesson for all Christians and for all Church leaders. "Wherever there is the Spirit of the Lord, there is liberty" (2Cor 3:17). On November 9, 1989, I was in Berlin, in front of the broken wall. With my piece of wood as violin I played a duet with Mstislav Rostropovich for the poor and the oppressed of all times, a melody of Helder Camara for a more just world:

> When one dreams alone,
> His dream is there forlorn;
> When many people dream,
> A new world is born.

When will all the walls, of whatever kind, finally learn to dance?

Brothers and sisters, politicians and simple people of Europe, I ask you to accept these words of exhortation, a greeting and thanksgiving from your poor little brother Francis, a citizen of Europe and of the world, standing at this moment on the high plateau of Guatemala. In 1992 on the wings of Brother Wind, I shall fly to Santo Domingo to commemorate the five hundred years of evangelization of the Americas; that year should also mark the beginning of a real discovery of Europe and its true values. Later on I would like to accompany the Lord Pope to Moscow and to Beijing.

I salute you all, in East and West, in North and South, with these words of exhortation and consolation which I heard last year in Dresden and in Prague, words that I have sung with the native peoples of Chichicastenango during these latter months:

Hope is everlasting:
Learn that as you stride.
And as you go on learning
Hope will be your guide.

January 1, 1992

27. How the worldwide brotherhood received new evangelical impulses through the intercession of St. Anthony of Padua

Background: The following text gathers impressions and experiences from several journeys.

About the time of the paschal solemnity in the year 1992, after much travel on many pilgrimages by water, on land, and in the air, the Minister withdrew to a hilly hermitage in order to do penance, to devote himself to the contemplative dimension, and there to meditate on the signs of life, death, and resurrection in the history of our brotherhood. And behold, it suddenly became clear to him that after being elected Minister General the previous year on the feast of the blessed Brother Anthony of Padua, he had in fact encountered this universal saint in the most wonderful way during the first months of his service. Some of these encounters are here set forth quite simply for the edification of others.

On the very first day of his service as Minister General, Brother Hermann received from Brother Anthony, the minister of the Province of the Holy Name in New York, the sad news that armed robbers had on the wonder-worker's own feastday stolen several thousand dollars from the cashbox of the shrine of St. Anthony on 31st Street, money which was destined for feeding many hundreds of poor people. Immediately the indignation among the citizens and their feelings of sympathy for the robbed friars were so great that in an action of solidarity spurred on by that state's governor, they collected in one week a sum of money twice as great as that which had been taken from the friars. The ministers and servants in faraway San Diego, upon hearing of this, wondered and asked themselves what such a sign might mean for the six-year period just begun, for example, for the fund-raising project which they had just approved.

Then at the start of the academic year, the Minister hurried to the Roman center of studies, the Antonianum, and there had explained to him by the brothers how the institution could be further renewed and how it could render an ever better qualified service in the evangelization of cultures. In a brief statement entitled *A Future for Our Past*, he then spoke of how the brotherhood rightly desires to pursue studies at a high scientific level, but it should not forget at the same time that, according to the example of the Doctor of the Church Anthony of Padua, witnesses to the faith are more important than masters, poets and prophets are more important than advocates of the past, visionaries are more important than administrators of the status quo. He spoke of how from the *memoria* of the past there must constantly grow a new *prophetia*, for as in the Holy Eucharist, from the dynamic memory of the past there grows the certainty of a new life in the future.

The Minister concluded with these words: "We can summon the courage to be at least little prophets, that is to say 'minor prophets.' And that means for a university which bears the name of Anthony to face the questions of today, the new questions concerning the life of humanity and of the cosmos; to place the human being before the Sabbath; not only to recognize and study the truth but also to do it; not to mistake the penultimate questions for the ultimate ones; to connect in our lives divine service and service of the poor; to make possible a multiplicity of voices in the concert of theology and spirituality." He concluded, "A vital multiplicity is the best guarantee for any lasting unity."

As the new liturgical year began, there was great indignation and confusion throughout Italy and among all those who had a special devotion to St. Anthony because one of the saint's most precious relics, a piece of the jawbone which enabled him to preach to so many people, had been stolen by shameless robbers from the basilica in Padua. Tireless were the investigations of the Carabinieri, countless were the prayers and the intercessions of the faithful. When the police finally found the precious relic in a wonderful way on a green lawn in Latium, the Minister experienced another sign of the care and protection which the *Doctor Mirabilis* had clearly wanted to bestow upon him ever since his election on June 13, 1991. A general of the Carabinieri, unaware of the wonderful multiplicity within the Franciscan family, confided to the

Minister General the happy news of the recovered relic. He offered to bring it immediately and solemnly to the Gelsomino Hill. The Minister first thanked the gentleman, praised the protectors of public order, but declined to receive the relic since it belonged traditionally to other brothers of the same Francis. It was then, in fact, solemnly returned to Padua in the Venice region. All the same, some brothers suspect that perhaps St. Anthony himself wanted to come to the curia of the Lesser Brothers on the Gelsomino in Rome in order to bring a special blessing upon all who lived there.

In the first weeks of the new calendar year, the Minister set out on a journey to Brazil in order to visit the brothers and with them give thanks on the occasion of the 500th anniversary of the evangelization of their continent while at the same time undertaking an examination of conscience. On the way there he was forced, "for technical reasons" he was told, to wait one day—a Tuesday—in Lisbon in a manner quite unforeseen and unplanned before he could continue his journey on the wings of the wind. So he begged hospitality and a simple lodging for the night from Brother Mario, the minister of the Province in Lusitania. Both petitions were granted him. Brother Mario showed him Varatojo's historic friary dedicated to St. Anthony as well as Lisbon's St. Anthony Friary, which is built on the spot where the saint was born. After the Minister had prayed there in the grotto, he gave to many of the brothers and sisters of the Franciscan family an address, based on a passage from the sermons of the great preacher:

> Whoever is Guardian and Minister of others must be distinguished by a pure life and by knowledge of the holy Scriptures. He must be able to express himself well, clearly and with conviction. He must be zealous in prayer and show a sympathetic understanding in his relations with others, for he must some day give a reckoning for those who have been entrusted to him. In everything he must have the golden gift of mildness and gentleness. He should be the father and the mother of all (Sermones).

With the great teachers of his brotherhood in mind, the Universal Minister also quoted a saying of William Faulkner who wrote: "The past is never dead. It is not even past." He ended by wishing all of them after the example of St. Antony of Lisbon "a clear head, a merry heart, a humble disposition." Thereupon he continued his journey.

Having reached the land under the Southern Cross, he realized that in Recife he had entered the territory of a province dedicated to the Saint of Lisbon and Padua. The Minister who greeted him likewise bore the name Antônio. In Olinda, where the young brothers are introduced to Franciscan life and into sacred theology, the Minister spoke with the assembled friars about the priorities of Franciscan studies. He encouraged all of them to serve an evangelization which speaks of hunger for bread and hunger for God at the same time, neither separating them nor confusing them. He mentioned that St. Anthony himself had shown an integral understanding of mission since in his theology, which was expressly praised by Brother Francis (EpAnt), the bread of Scripture and of the Eucharist may not be separated from the bread of the hungry and of the poor since both of them are the expression of God's single love and the sacrament of his preferential option for humanity.

The Minister pointed out that according to both the ancient and the modern masters of the brotherhood, it is of no importance simply to amass a great deal of knowledge. The wise man is rather the one who is able to apply his knowledge for the benefit of others and for the service of the world. Finally he told them what he had discovered in Portugal about the pedagogical method of St. Anthony. A novice had left the fraternity in which Anthony was teaching. It seemed that life according to the Gospel was too burdensome for the young man. Secretly he took with him a valuable book of Psalms, which was of great importance for the fraternity. Brother Anthony had copied in it his precious notes. Led by the Saint, they all prayed fervently to the Lord, and their prayer was heard. Not only did the former novice contritely bring back the book, he also asked to be readmitted to obedience and became for the many years of his long life an exemplary Lesser Brother.

By way of Fortaleza, where he visited a certain Cardinal Aloysius, who many years before had been a professor at the Roman Antonianum, the Minister arrived at S. Luiz do Maranhâo, where between 1624 and 1706 the brothers from Portugal had a Custody of St. Anthony. In this place also a certain Brother Antônio Vieira (1608-1697), who it must be said was a member of the Society of Jesus, preached against the avarice of some colonizers and the immorality of the slave traders, thereby showing himself to be a precursor of an authentic theology of liberation. This great missionary positioned himself on the coast of the Atlantic Ocean and preached to the fishes because hard-hearted men would not listen to him. This is similar to what we read about the Blessed Anthony at Rimini on the Adriatic (Fior 60).

In the year 1952 missionaries had come from the Saxony province to continue these Gospel traditions and to implant the Franciscan life here once more. Since that time so many young brothers from the "basic ecclesial communities" had been admitted to obedience that a new Vice-Province could be erected. On the feast of the Epiphany of the Lord, the Minister read out the official Roman decree. And on the evening of that same day, a young man of that country made profession of his final vows into the hands of the Brother Minister from Rome as a sign that a new branch had begun to grow on the trunk of the worldwide brotherhood. And the name of this young friar was Antônio Pacheco.

In the weeks which followed, the Minister again came across his patron saint in several places: in the friary of S. Antônio in Belo Horizonte, where before a large gathering of sisters and brothers he spoke about the priorities of evangelization today; in Sao Paulo, where he spoke with a certain Brother Leonardo about the student years they shared in the Province of St. Anthony in Bavaria and about the obligation they shared in the name of the Church and of the brotherhood to live the spirit of the Saint also in new forms, particularly among the poor; in San Francisco in California, where every day in the name of Brother Anthony thousands of the hungry are fed, the naked are clothed, the sick are healed, the suffering are consoled; in Bologna in Emilia Romagna, where a certain Brother Ernesto, founder of the social center called "Antoniano," celebrated his golden jubilee of priesthood; in Laç in cold Albania, where with the help of this same Brother Ernesto from the Antoniano of Bologna, as well as with the support and help even of the Muslims of Albania, a sanctuary of St. Anthony, which the former holders of government power had shamelessly destroyed, is being rebuilt. For all these encounters and moments of illumination the Minister thanked the Lord.

Thereafter Brother Hermann resolved to visit Brazil again on the first anniversary of his election as Minister General, on the occasion of the United Nations conference on ecology and cosmic survival. On the Praça Mahatma Gandhi, in front of our friary Santo Antônio in Rio de Janeiro, it was his desire to pray and fast together with innumerable sisters and brothers from the whole Franciscan family. Moreover he wanted to join with many people of goodwill in calling on the universal Saint, the wonder-worker, the finder of lost objects of value, and the creator of new perspectives, Antony of Lisbon-Padua-Rio-Rome. He prayed that, through the intercession of St. Anthony, the millions of poor might at last be given human dignity and bread; that the powerful of this world might make peace with one another and with the martyred world; that the many children forced to live on open streets and squares might find a home; that all those in need might be given a new vision of a just world order; and, finally, that the Franciscan family might ever more clearly take up the ministry and *diakonia* (service) of peacemaking as the necessary consequence of its faith in the Risen Lord, preaching it after the example of Francis and Anthony more by deeds than by words.

Monte Paolo, April 26, 1992

28. Concerning a fraternal visit by the Minister to the savannas by the Zambezi River

Background: At the end of June 1992 there took place in Lusaka (Zambia) the official opening of a new Inter-Franciscan Study Center run by the Friars Minor (OFM), the Capuchins (OFMCap), and the Conventuals (OFMConv). The three Ministers General, Flavio Carraro (OFMCap), Lanfranco Serrini (OFMConv), and H. Schalück (OFM) were present.

In the middle of the year of the Lord 1992 while war was still raging in the heart of Europe and Southern Africa was experiencing a struggle for peace and equal rights, the Minister set on a journey to the land by the Zambezi River with its Victoria Falls. He was accompanied by Brothers Peter and Sebastiao. In the cool of the dawn of an African winter morning, they finally entered the road named after the Blue Boar, leading to the new St. Bonaventure Center not far from the capital, Lusaka, in the suburb Makeni. There they were warmly greeted by brothers from many tribes and nations, surrounded by a reddish-yellow cloud of dust thrown up by their vehicle in the shimmering light of the dry Central African plateau. They had come to inaugurate a study and formation center, called after the Doctor Seraphicus from Bagnoregio, which was now to serve the whole Franciscan family. Before them, Brother

Flavio and Brother Lanfranco, Ministers of the other two Orders taking part, had already arrived, also traveling from their curias near the Tiber. The new center was to be, in the mind of all those taking part, a sign of the common task of implanting the brotherhood permanently in those regions of the continent, to give the universal Brother Francis an African face, and to help overcome forever a tribal mentality, not only in Africa but even in Rome. Everyone was convinced more than ever that under the one Lord of History there ought to be only brothers and sisters and that under the one Francis of Assisi there should be only brothers and sisters of a single family.

To their joy all the visitors from Rome were able to see that in fact the new common center was designed in such a way that it expressed in its various elements, "unmixed and yet unified," like the Blessed Trinity, at one and the same time unity and plurality. All three groups kept their own identity spatially and even canonically, having their own fraternities. At the same time they contributed to a new reality in the common Eucharist, mutual respect and brotherly love, made visible to all in a common church and a common *Aula Magna* (Great Hall). They also shared other rooms, in which all the friars together were instructed in manual work and in sacred theology. Their common library contained learned works not only from the Middle Ages but also from modern times, with manuscripts and printed works not only from the city named eternal and holy but also from Brazil and Britain—yes even from distant and exotic Germany. And during a solemn religious service when the sound of drums and of the songs of the brothers and of the simple people who had hurried there was carried out far into the high lands, the three Ministers blessed the rooms large and small of the new African school and the library. Then each one blessed those rooms in which the fraternity of his own Order would be living.

In his homily Brother Hermann pointed out that even allowing for every erudition, the true academy and school of a Lesser Brother in Orient or Occident, in North or South, is the leprosarium and life with the poor. During the preparation of the gifts, Brother Flavio was presented with a live chicken, Brother Lanfranco with a basket of yellow maize, and Brother Hermann with a sack of tapioca roots. After the Eucharistic celebration all refreshed themselves with rice, beans, cooked chicken, bananas, and millet beer, brought by neighbors in sufficient quantities. In the evening everyone met for an interfranciscan and international recreation.

Once more there sounded out rhythms which had never been heard on the Gelsomino Hill in Rome; the young brothers demonstrated to their formators and Ministers how they imagined Francis and Clare with an African face. The finale came with the singing by all the African brothers together, lighting up the black African night for a moment with its stirring harmonies, of W. A. Mozart's setting of *Venerabilis Barba Cappuccinorum*.

In order to recover from the fatigue of curial sittings and nocturnal travels, the Minister felt the need of engaging in some sport as he often did in the Gelsomino. So he let it be known that he wanted to take a run over the high land every day for half an hour or so. Two brothers from Mozambique promptly offered to accompany him in this. One was called Samuel, the other was named Kisito after one of the Uganda martyrs. So the three of them trotted off through the noonday heat of the savanna, over dry grass, thistles, and thorny undergrowth, avoiding snakes and scorpions. Children hurried out of their huts at the sight of this unusual spectacle and clapped their hands with delight; tired dogs, disturbed in their afternoon sleep, yelped wearily; many-colored birds peeped inquisitively out of the branches of a breadfruit tree, and a gazelle, disturbed at her peaceful grazing, scampered off hastily into the bushes. The two young brothers tended to run faster than the Minister, showing him the way and calling his attention to obstacles while putting questions to him and giving him advice for his universal ministry. A little breathless, but purified and refreshed in body and spirit, the Minister returned with his companions and guardians to the Bonaventure Center in Makeni.

During those days there occurred in Lusaka a seminar in which the three Ministers General presented their "Priorities and Hopes" in the realm of formation and studies of their own fraternities and encouraged all to live the Franciscan insight in their own continent with great fidelity but also with great creativity. The Ministers said that the African sisters and brothers of St. Francis, while remaining true to their own peoples and cultures, should at the same time, through their own experiences and insights, help the whole Church and the entire Franciscan movement towards a wider catholicity. The young brothers for their part shared the following insights with their Ministers: the members of the Franciscan family, whether men or women, whether contemplatives or wandering preachers, must be a sign of the Kingdom to come by their inner unity and solidarity in the service of evangelization;

the brothers and sisters throughout the whole world, whatever the color and form of their habits or of their skins, should see in the crucified Jesus the center of the Church and in the poor the sacrament of Christ; the poor, including those in Africa, no longer wanted to be "objects" of evangelization, but saw themselves as "subjects" of liberation in the name of the Lord of History; and the foremost Franciscan service in the cause of liberation is not the giving of alms but the fight for justice and for the chance of life for all, with a reconciled heart. In conclusion, the African brothers thanked the Ministers for having come not only to talk but also to listen and to learn from the young brothers—without complaining about the cold nights, the dust, and the unevenness of the savannas by the Zambezi River. After that the three Ministers returned to Rome by different ways, thankful for having experienced firsthand the truth of the African proverb: "A great many arms and hands are needed to encompass a breadfruit tree."

Rome, July 15, 1992

29. Why the brothers' curia in Rome is built upon a hill fragrant with the scent of jasmine

Background: To understand this text, it is important to know that the hill upon which the General Curia of the Franciscan Order in Rome is built is popularly called the "Gelsomino," the Italian word for jasmine.

On a Mediterranean spring evening in the mild month of May, after a tiring pilgrimage which took him to the brothers in Lima and in Ayacucho in the Cordilleras of distant Peru, as well as to the Virgen Morena de Guadalupe in Mexico, the Minister returned to his hill named after jasmine *(Gelsomino)* in the center of the city called eternal and holy. As he turned into the narrow cul-de-sac named after the Mediatrix of All Graces, which leads up to the Roman curia of his worldwide brotherhood, he recalled a saying of the indigenous people of the Andes. They had said to him as they bade farewell: "The poor people love your brothers, whose brown robes remind us every day of the color of our Mother Earth, our ancestral *Pachamama* who has always been good to us." Why should it not be possible, he wondered, for the whole brotherhood to look with new, clear eyes at the earth and upon everything growing upon it, in order to have a fresher and clearer understanding of their mission? As this thought crossed his mind, his nostrils were greeted by the friendly and seductive scent of the plants which had been growing here peacefully since time immemorial, offspring of the *Jasminum odoratissimum* of the Canary Islands and the hills of Provence, of the *Jasminum grandiflorum* from the region of the distant Himalayas and inaccessible Kashmir, of the *Jasminum officinale* from mysterious Iran, the Bismarck Archipelago and the Pacific Islands of the Sondas, of the *Jasminum nudiflorum* from the Middle Kingdom in the Far East. In the end he recognized also the unmistakable *Gelsomino della Madonna* or *Philadelphus coronarius* which apparently originated in Umbria, Morocco, and the Near East, but from the start did not want to be absent from the brotherhood's center. And the Minister asked himself and others what indication the jasmine might give for the path to be followed by his Order and for its evangelizing mission. Not least, there was a mysterious statement made by the poet Gabriel García Marquez, which he had once heard from a young brother in Colombia and which now also made him curious: "You are really grown up when you have discovered that jasmine is a flower that opens up only in the night."

When in those spring days there arrived in the curia the members of a commission to elaborate a new *Ratio Evangelisationis*, there were represented from Occident and Orient, from the Northern and from the Southern Hemispheres, from the periphery and from the center, as many lands, experiences, fragrances, and colors as there were among the jasmine plants growing outside the house. And the Minister opened the first session with the saying of the great Wise One of China: "If you carry in your heart a branch of blossom, very soon it will become the perch for a singing bird." The Lesser Brothers, wherever they are, he explained, should in evangelizing by word and example make use of such fragrant words, such colorful metaphors, such new songs, that they succeed like Brother Anthony at the Chapter of Arles in making Francis himself visibly present (1Cel 18).

The Minister reminded them that the new evangelization presupposes a new culture of silence and of contemplation, "that we may not be found among those who possess the fine art of using many words to say nothing." He said that the scent of both the exotic and the ordinary jasmine reminds us of what Albert Einstein wrote: "The deepest and finest experience possible for a human being is that of mystery. This is the basis for all the others,

including those of art and science." It also reminds us of the deep
conviction of our Father and Brother Francis that we must be
converted ourselves before we can preach to others. Finally, it
reminds us of the sayings of innumerable mystics, ancient and new,
known by name or anonymous, who tell us that music and fragrance
are the truly distinctive signs of the new person and the new world.
He reminded them that the visions of today will be the realities of
tomorrow and concluded his encouragement for a creative reflection
with these words:

> Show your love for the rainbow and the butterfly,
>   the precious flower, the wild jasmine,
>   the heavens filled with stars, and the dreams
>   which are not afraid of becoming realities.
> Because a love which is not expressed
>   is like a candle not allowed to show its light,
>   or a melody not allowed to be sounded.

In those years the curia on the Jasmine Hill was making an
effort to become more and more an international fraternity.
Therefore everyone thought it important to learn, besides the Latin
language, new languages like Swahili, Thai, and Russian; besides
Gregorian chants, also the new rhythms and melodies expressive of
every culture and nation; and besides the art of using words, also
the art of silence, of painting, of music, and of dance so that
multiplicity might shine through our unity and unity through our
multiplicity. That is why the jasmine is esteemed by the brothers
not only for its common root but also for its innumerable blossoms
and scents coming from a variety of climes and seasons.

Moreover in the course of the years, apart from the jasmine as a
symbol of friendly hospitality, they had managed to make other
herbs and plants grow and flourish on what had once been a barren
hill—the sycamore tree, whose top incidentally makes a perfect
observation point (Lk 19:4); the ever-green myrtle, with its dark
gloss and fine aroma, which in the messianic age, according to the
prophet Isaiah (41:19; 55:13) will grow even in the desert and in
places where before only nasty stinging nettles could flourish; the
thorny but very useful furze, whose shadow is sought by people in
the desert (1Kg 19:4-5) and whose roots are edible (Job 30:4); palms
from every continent; cypress, oak, and terebinth, thyme, hibiscus,
and fiery rhododendron, the almond tree which in the spring is the
first to flower and whose name in Hebrew means "watchful" (Jer
1:11-12); the rose and the common lily in the field (Mt 6:28); even

various cacti from the deserts of Arizona and Nevada; but above all the olive tree, sign of eschatological bliss (Hos 2:24), of happiness in sorrow, of fruitfulness in sterility, of perseverance in affliction. In the garden of the curia on the Gelsomino Hill there grew thus many a gnarled olive tree as a symbol of respect (Ps 23:5), of friendship, and of the bond of brothers (Ps 133:2). It reminded the friars every day of their evangelical service of salvation, liberation, consolation, and support for the poor.

In this same month of May there was observed in the Curia its matronal feast, the Mediatrix of all Graces, in which all prayed for the maternal protection of the *rosa mystica,*. The Minister was joined in a solemn celebration by many bishops from the Republic of South Africa who had found for a few weeks humble quarters in the shade of the jasmine because, owing to great celebrations in St. Peter's, there was no place for them in other Roman hostels. An archbishop from distant Lesotho later wrote about the Jasmine Hill, applying the words of Celano: "The earth resounded with mighty voices, the air was filled with rejoicings, and the ground was moistened with tears of joy. New songs were sung, and the servants of God gave expression to their joy in melody of spirit. Sweet sounding organs were heard there and spiritual hymns were sung with well modulated voices. There a very sweet odor was breathed, and a more joyous melody that stirred the emotions resounded there. The day was bright and colored with more splendid rays than usual. There were green olive branches and fresh branches of other trees there . . . and the blessing of peace filled the minds of those who had come there with joy" (1Cel 126).

Shortly before the feast of St. Anthony, before the Minister finally traveled to Rio for the Global Forum about the protection of the environment and universal justice, he called together several brothers and sisters in order to listen to their counsel and so prepare himself better for an address he was to give in that place. They all concurred in saying that the message of Brother Francis to today's threatened world is not to be found only in books or on learned Roman parchments and decrees but also in hearing the sighs of afflicted creation and the cry of the poor.

But more particularly it is to be found in the mysterious music of the universe, in the scent of bread and roses, of oleander and the common jasmine. Together they wondered what duty the Lord of History would want to place today upon his Church and upon the Franciscan family through the example of St. Francis, who in his own time had healed a leper in body and soul with precious aromatic spices (Fior 25). Did Francis not bring to mind the teaching method of Jesus, which consisted in allowing wheat and tares to grow together, impartially, without fuss, and in sending his rain on the righteous and the sinner alike? Was he not, as it were, a constant and friendly reminder for the brothers and sisters everywhere to acquire not only a love for computers and photocopiers but also the capacity for lending an attentive ear, for dialogue, and for fraternal correction? Did he not caution us to take pleasure not so much in the sound of mighty horns, trumpets, and big drums, but rather in the gentle, peace-inducing sound of harps and zithers; to admire not only the flight of the eagle, but also that of the butterfly and the gray sparrow; to prefer contemplating not only exotic orchids but also the hidden beauty of furze and common thistle? They saw more clearly than ever that what is really important in everything, and therefore also in the service of peace, is to understand and pass on the "fragrant words of our Lord" (EpFid 2) and in everything to recognize and adore the Creator "for his own sake."

Did Francis not give a strict command that in every vegetable garden a piece of earth should be reserved for sweet-smelling plants and flowers so that all those who saw them should praise the Creator and be brought to "the memory of the Eternal Sweetness" (2Cel 124)? Thus they thought that in Rio the Minister should say that we can heal the earth only if we first heal and purify ourselves. We should learn to acknowledge our guilt and not lose heart, knowing that the tears of pain and penitence often water the tenderest and prettiest of flowers. Speaking as a little brother the Minister wanted to call to the mighty ones of the world: "I do not want to count as my friend anyone who needlessly tramples underfoot a single worm." He would tell his hearers everywhere about the Roman and the universal jasmine which prefers to flower by night. As for himself, he wanted to be reminded often of a saying which he had heard from the Iroquois: "Perform your service quietly and in silence; words only rob it of all effect."

By way of conclusion, Brother Gilles, the Vicar of the worldwide brotherhood, addressed to the Minister and all the others present the following words of exhortation:

> If I were to speak in the tongue of curias and diplomats,
>   and were rich in knowledge but poor in wisdom;

If I were to prefer the logic of power to the logic of a
vulnerable blossom,
I would become but withered wood and a shriveled flower.
But the fruits of the spirit are sensitivity, self-criticism,
humor, recognition of one's own limitations,
unconditional solidarity with the powerless,
but also the ability to distinguish
when a person's survival depends on a piece of bread,
and when for the poor it is rather
a rose or a gentle melody that is important."

Thereupon the Minister set out on his travels on the dewy
morning of a day in spring, once more leaving behind for a time the
Gelsomino Hill but continuing to carry in his heart its unforgettable
message.

Rome, August 23, 1992

30. A reflection on justice, peace, and the integrity of creation

*Background: The following text arose in connection with the
discussion about peace, justice, and the safeguarding of creation and
about Franciscan responses to crisis situations around the world.
John Quigley, OFM and James Perluzzi, OFM (both in Rome) and
the author discussed possible responses. This text grew out of that
discussion.*

It was the year of our Lord 1992. All over the world countless
utopias envisioned by countless people of goodwill were once again
being trodden into the sand, as had happened shortly before in the
Gulf War. More and more people came to recognize ever more
clearly that wars have never resolved problems but serve only to
create new ones. Some governments were at war with each other
while the peoples and above all the mothers and the poor of the
world in thousands of streets and squares demanded that
investment should be made in life instead of financing senseless
killing. Increasingly, precious and chaste water was being violated
by the obscene acts of war. Some still spoke of the need for
"surgically clean" bombing missions. In the meantime, undimmed
and destructive hatred consumed the hearts of many people and
darkened their minds.

But there were also many men and women of diverse lands and
religions who asked themselves and each other how the world,

and indeed the whole cosmos, could still be rescued from the avarice and destructive madness of humanity. A well-known theologian of the Roman Church had just brought together his inquiries in a new book in which he pointed out insistently to the whole world: "There can never be peace among peoples without peace and without reconciliation among religions." Many centuries before, a German cardinal and theologian who also spent much of his life in Rome, namely, Nicolas of Cusa (1401-1464), had expressed similar thoughts in his writing *De Pace seu Concordantia Fidei*. In 1453, as Constantinople was being captured by the Turks, he wrote: "You it is, O Lord, Giver of Being and of Life, who while always remaining one and the same God, are called in various ways and with various names in various religions. . . . Do not hide any longer. Then will rest the sword and all hate and all suffering, and all people will come to see that in the variety of religious usages there is only one religion *(una religio in rituum varietate)*."

And behold, even in the Roman curia of the Lesser Brothers on the secure Gelsomino Hill a holy restlessness was in the air. The question was asked ever more insistently about what should be the future priorities and options of the brotherhood. In obedience to Brother Francis and not least also in obedience to the Lord Pope, who in those months, in contrast with the wise and clever of this world and in contrast with the "Realpolitik" of the great ones, had not ceased to denounce the senselessness of war, they asked themselves urgently whether the time had not come to attempt a new initiative in the work for peace, worldwide justice, and the safeguarding of creation. They saw this task as a Franciscan service for the evangelization of the world and as a small contribution to a better future and a lasting peace.

To understand better the saying of Gandhi that nonviolence is not something for weak but for brave hearts, in the wild month of March, the Minister journeyed to the Nevada desert. There he met a group of sisters and brothers who are convinced that the very production of violence through weapons, especially atomic weapons, is already a theft from the poor of the whole world. For many years this group, led by a certain Louis, a former minister of the Province in California, has appealed to the conscience of the world and of its leaders in order to remind all humanity of the priority of life over death. They also reminded the brotherhood of its obligation to praise and worship the Lord of life and not to follow false gods. In the gray light of morning as the sun was rising over the desert, all those who had come for the Lenten Desert

Experience took part in a liturgy of the word and of the bread. During it they all prayed to be found worthy to proclaim to the whole world and to the whole cosmos the Good News of its redemption, of welcome to new life. They sought to do this in such a way that the whole mystery of Christ, his death and resurrection, but also the priority of life over death would shine out (GC 100).

In his homily Brother Hermann spoke about "allowing ourselves to be touched and saved by the God of peace and of mercy before we can heal the earth." At the moment of the breaking of bread, he recalled the commission of Christ to keep alive in the midst of a culture of death and of war the living memory of the God who does not want to destroy the world and its life but instead seeks to bring it to perfection. And all listened attentively to the song which a Native American of the Shonas tribe sang to his own words and melody giving expression to both lament and hope:

O great Spirit, whose voice I hear in the winds and whose breath gives life to the entire world, hear me. I come before you as one of your children. I am small and weak. I have need of your strength and wisdom. Let me wander among beauty and let my eyes always see the purple-red setting of the sun. Let my hands respect the things you have made and let my ears hear your voice. Grant me the wisdom to discover the teaching you have hidden in the desert, in every leaf and in every rock and in every peaceful person.

After this, Brother Hermann desired to discover more precisely what was being done in the brotherhood for the priority of the service of peace and active nonviolence in obedience to the Lord Pope. The Minister was always conscious that while he must be attentive to the concerns of the brotherhood's curia, there must also be a time for pilgrimage and for life with the brothers wherever they live. That is to say the brotherhood's leaders need time for "defining" and analyzing ideas and the experiences gathered, but also time for gathering completely *new* experiences and challenges in unaccustomed circumstances and marginal situations still to be defined, which the Seraphic Doctor St. Bonaventure had called "speculation of a poor man in the desert" (*Itinerarium*).

And so he set out in the hot month of June for the United Nations World Summit on the Environment. There at the Global Forum in Rio de Janeiro he learned a great deal about many experiences in the service of peace, justice, and the conservation of the environment. On Mahatma Gandhi Square he celebrated with the Franciscan family an ecumenical liturgy, during which everyone sang:

> The dying forests look to us, the polluted seas and rivers
>   have need of our constancy.
> The parched desert and the denuded hills look to us,
>   the dying flora and fauna
>   have need of our constancy.
> People who have been exploited and cheated of life
>   look to us in all the continents
>   and have need of our constancy and solidarity.
> We look at each other and ask:
> Will we find ways for love, understanding for
>   the God who loves life,
>   hope for mankind and for the cosmos?
> Will the peace of God once more let the world grow green,
>   let all the deserts of the world become alive
>   not with weapons and walls and barriers
>   but with oases and prophets,
> Will it people again the dead oceans
>   and let us smile once more without fear?

At a press conference which he later gave together with sisters and brothers from various countries, the Minister spoke of the priority of active love, of "political diakonia," as certain theologians have called it, over the Scripture scholars' analysis of the Law (Lk 10). The brothers did not want to be like those who would like to learn to swim without having to go into the water. Therefore in obedience to their General Constitutions they wanted to seek dialogue with all religions (93:1) since, as is becoming more and more clear to them, the traces and seeds of the one Word of God are to be found in all religions and cultures (93:2) and precisely where the great ones of this world least expect it. And with special solicitude, following the desire of St. Francis, they wanted to encounter the brothers and sisters of Islam (95:3). In everything they wanted to be guided by good experiences and not by bad ones. Brother Hermann said that his visit to the Global Forum and to the poor people of the country had led him to recognize the truth of Albert Einstein's saying: "We must be prepared to make the same sacrifices in the cause of peace as we have made without hesitation in the cause of war."

Shortly before Advent in the year 1992, the Minister General, accompanied by Brothers Emmanuel and John, went to visit the regions and Provinces in Croatia, Bosnia, and Herzegovina. They wanted to give their Franciscan brothers afflicted by the war there, as well as all men and women of goodwill, a sign of their support and solidarity. They met the brothers in Split, Zagreb, Dubvrovnik, Tomislavgrad, Livno, and in many other places. They also paid a fraternal visit to the bishop of Mostar and the cardinal of Zagreb.

The Minister visited the wounded, comforted the refugees, listened to words of lament, desperation, and hope. Repeatedly they sang the *Magnificat*, according to which the mighty will be cast from their thrones and the lowly raised up. He told of other people's suffering and example in South Africa, Somalia, China, and Peru, speaking of the solidarity needed in suffering as well as in hope. He then read from the new General Constitutions, which they had all solemnly promised to observe, for himself and for all the brothers, these words: "Conscious also of the atrocious dangers threatening humanity, the Brothers must firmly *denounce* every species of warlike action and the armament race as a very grave plague upon the world and an extremely serious injustice towards the poor. Let them not spare any energy or omit any effort to build up the Kingdom of peace" (69:2). He spoke also of his conviction that one day not too far away, war as a means of policy will be as outmoded and despised as slavery, colonialism, and the oppression of women.

All of them begged the Lord for the courage to dream the great vision of God's Kingdom, in which no people will any longer live at the cost of any other and to be given the even greater courage to take the first tiny and modest steps towards it, as is appropriate for Lesser Brothers. Inspired by the new vision which had been proposed to them by the Pentecost Chapter, the Minister at the end of his visit called out to the brothers:

No one showed us what we had to do,
    but the Lord himself revealed during these years
    to his fraternity
    in old and new signs
    that they were to live in the manner of the
    kenosis of Jesus
    and of his active nonviolence,
    to serve the peace and the life of the world and
    of the whole cosmos
    and to make greater sacrifices for a culture

of peace and reconciliation
than are made for a culture of rivalry,
power and blasphemous war,
which disfigures the name and the face of our Lord.
And the brothers are strictly bound by obedience
to listen to the poor, the powerless,
and the victims of war,
instead of interpreting the world and its history
through the eyes and hearts
of the victors and the mighty.
For the Lord shows his power in the powerless.
And the brothers should not so much ask
how they can evangelize others,
as first to let themselves be evangelized
by the peace-loving, the poor, and the
victims of exploitation, apartheid, racism, and war.
For it is not victory *in* war and supremacy over others
which will bring peace to the world,
but only victory *over* war
and a life of respect for others
and of service of one another.
If we want to remain faithful to the
charism of our Father and Brother,
we must be prepared for a radical conversion
and first live in ourselves peace, justice,
and reverence for creation,
in order then to proclaim to others
the peace of God.

Then they all returned to Rome to the Gelsomino Hill.

Rome, January 1, 1993

Chapter 5
1993-1994

1993

31. Monologue of a gray donkey from the Upper Nile

Background: During a visit to Upper Egypt in January 1993 the Minister General, following a custom of Oriental hospitality, entered a Christian village on the back of a donkey.

My name is Mustafa. I am three years old and have never left my village of Rezegat on the Upper Nile in Egypt. Up to now I have been allowed to carry only "the cucumbers, the melons, the leeks, the onions, and the garlic" (Nm 11:5) to market. Children and old people love to ride on my back to the Nile. But today must surely be a special day. We have guests. No, not a family in flight as on that occasion many centuries ago. Only the Minister of the Franciscans from Rome. The villagers lead him in solemn procession through the village to the church. How the children are enthusiastically waving their palm-fans! My passenger is sitting unsteadily on my back and Brother Adel, the minister of Egypt, is very concerned that he could lose his balance.

It is quite unjust to think of us donkeys as sullen and obstinate. If it were so, why did our Lord and Brother Jesus, on the only occasion on which he wanted to ride, get onto a donkey and not onto a proud horse (Jn 12:15)? So I comfort myself with the saying of the Father of the Church, St. Ambrose, who went so far as to put forward the donkey as a model for people: "Learn from the donkey how Jesus should be carried. . . . Learn willingly to offer him the back of your spirit. Learn to be under Christ, so that you may be over the world" *(Sermones).* And while it is true that Brother Francis forbade his friars to ride, this was only on the back of the proud horse (RegB). By contrast, he gave his full trust to the simple, gray donkey. For he often rode on the back of one of us, particularly when he was sick and weary (2Cel 31). Is it not true to say that he made a kind of "preferential option for the gray donkey," faithful in this to the example of the Lord, who himself was to ride into Jerusalem on a donkey and there proclaim peace and justice for all, as foretold by one of the minor prophets (Zec 9:9-10)?

The Minister from Rome arrived an hour ago at the airport of Luxor in a modern jet airliner, coming from Cairo. From there he was driven in a car as far as the entrance to the village. At that point small steps had been prepared for him so that he could comfortably climb onto my back. I have the sensation that our mode of transport, so usual in the lands between the Arab and the Libyan deserts, is unfamiliar to him. In fact, I think he is a bit apprehensive. Not like Brother Francis, who could go into ecstasy on the back of the donkey and give himself to the contemplative dimension, as he did once in Borgo San Sepolcro (2Cel 98).

But out of gratitude to Brother Francis, I will behave myself in a friendly way towards his successor—in a fraternal manner if I may be permitted the expression. Perhaps after all his tiring travels to the brothers and sisters in Catalonia, the Caucases, Cappadocia, Calabria, Kazakhstan, Kenya, Corea, Cuba, and Cologne, as also to the Greater and Lesser Antilles, I ought to remind him of the wise saying of that ancient author Horace: "The Via Appia is less taxing for those who are not in a hurry."

It has come to my ears that the day before yesterday Brother Hermann celebrated in faraway Cairo a festive liturgy, during which the young Brothers Michael and Hamdi made their solemn profession. There was a great gathering of people, and his sermon made the point, using the example of the mustard seed in the Gospel (Lk 13:18-19), that nothing is too small to prepare and foreshadow great things. Zacchaeus, so it is reported from this sermon, is another good example of how God entrusts great things to little beings. To me, too? During a meeting by the Pyramids of Ghiza, to which all the brothers from the Province of the Holy Family in Egypt had made their way, the Minister reported as follows from the life of the Order.

The great vision of the future Kingdom of peace and justice impels the brothers everywhere to undertake here and now the small steps of conversion and new evangelization which Brother Francis expects at all times from his brothers and sisters. He also spoke of the renewal of studies in the service of evangelization and of the growing interest in Eastern and Far Eastern languages. At the same time he warned all in the words of the *Legend of Perugia*: "Knowledge by itself puffs up. Love alone builds up" (*Scientia inflat, caritas autem aedificat*).

He went on to speak of his meeting with the Coptic Pope Shenouda in the desert monastery of Amba Bishoy, as well as with Sheik Giad-el-Hak, the head of the Muslims in our land, in his palace in the Medina of Cairo. And when questions were then put to him about the difficulties and the obstacles in the life of the brotherhood, he exclaimed: "A great Order cannot afford to be worried about little problems!" The great sage Mahatma Gandhi had said: "The true Christian has three qualities: he has no fear, he is always in the midst of difficulties, and in spite of that he is inexpressibly happy." I, Mustafa the donkey from the Upper Nile, think that it would be a good thing if our Minister and all his brothers remembered in all their large and small concerns the saying of Immanuel Kant: "There are three things which help us to bear the hardships of life: hope, sleep and laughter." He was indeed a great philosopher, as far as I can judge the matter.

Regarding Germany, I have discovered that my rider comes from that exotic part of the world, from the Paderborn Archdiocese. This brings to mind how John of Pian del Carpine, who was a minister in the Province of Saxony, on his missionary endeavors used to move about those inhospitable parts on the back of a donkey. "For the people at that time," so the learned chronicler Jordan of Giano remarks, "the Order was still new, and the humility of the rider was such that they were moved to a greater reverence for his donkey than is shown today for the person of a minister." A strange country, that transalpine Saxony. At any rate, John was a "courageous defender of his Order before bishops and princes" (Giano 55).

And what is the Minister going to say to the people, when in a few moments' time he reaches our humble village church? I wish I could suggest to him the following words:

> Good day, good people of Rezegat. My brothers have brought you the Gospel. You in turn are teaching us the evangelical option for the poor, who will possess the Kingdom of God. Our entry into your village here on the Upper Nile brings to mind not the palaces and the curias of the powerful, incense, ebony, leopard skins and purple, but rather the wisdom of the poor, the hope of the meek, the power of the peace-loving, the wisdom of those who bring about peace. Preserve the three treasures of which the sage Lao Tze spoke in distant China: the first is love, the second is moderation, the third is humility. Only one who loves has courage, only a person of moderation is generous, only the humble one is capable of exercising authority. It was of a Christian community such as Rezegat that a European

poet was thinking when he wrote: "Full many a Flower is born to blush unseen, and waste its Sweetness on the desert Air" (Thomas Gray). You have reminded us today of Jesus and Francis of Assisi and of the task that the Lord has in truth laid upon us, namely, to be brothers and sisters of the poor, to overcome evil with good, to be advocates of a culture of peace and solidarity. Pax et Bonum, Salaam, Shalom to every person and to every beast.

Before he dismounted my rider gently scratched my ear. Had he understood me? I hope so. In any case, tomorrow he will leave Rezegat, Cairo, Abu Simbel, Alexandria, Aswan, and its great waters, the Nile, the desert of Nubia, the oases, and all the sweet scents of the Near East as well as the Sphinx of Ghiza, get back into his jet, and return to his hill in Rome which exhales the fragrance of jasmine. May his brotherhood continue to remind the Church of the Lord not to put its trust in steeds and chariots, but in the name of the Lord (Ps 20:8) and in many a little gray donkey like myself.

Cairo, January 29, 1993

32. Concerning a journey of the Minister in Thailand

Background: *The occasion for this journey was the coming together for the biennial meeting of all the ministers provincial from Asia and Oceania, this time held at Udon Thani in northeast Thailand.*

While an intense cold was holding Old Europe in its grip and an absurd war was destroying lives and hopes in the Balkans, the Minister, Brother Hermann, decided to set out once more from Rome, from the city called eternal, and from the hill redolent of the sweet scent of jasmine. He, too, had heard the mysterious words "light from the East" and had resolved to travel on the wings of Brother Wind to Asia and Oceania in order to hold a fraternal meeting with all the ministers of that continent and its numerous islands. He was also moved by a strong desire to become better acquainted personally than had previously been possible with the cultures and religions of the East, which have so much to say to us about peace and humanity.

As he flew through the night above the lands of the Caucasus, Persia, and Kashmir, always in the direction of the rising sun, he fervently prayed the Lord of History to give him in Asia the opportunity of conversion and penance to enable him the more clearly to point out to the universal brotherhood the road of the future. Shortly before the majestic airplane bearing the name "St. Francis of Assisi" embraced the fertile soil of Thailand, the Minister laid aside for a moment the Roman breviary and prayed instead a psalm composed by an unknown poet of the isle of Kalimantan:

> You have created the continents, you have made men
>> diverse in language and culture.
> For man's sake you cause the rice and the bamboo to grow.
> It is you who show yourself to be the source of life
>> in all the diverse religions and cultures.
> It is you who are our God, good, peaceful,
>> merciful and compassionate.
> O Lord, grant a cessation to the mortal combat
>> between races, peoples and religions.
> Grant that everyone may become convinced
>> that they are brothers and sisters under the one God.
> Give peace to Asia and to the whole world.
> Give peace to the whole universe,
>> to the steppes and the forests,
>> to the seas and the shores.
> Give us pure eyes to see the beauty of your presence
>> and to love others.
> Lord, give us trust in one another;
>> above all give us the great ability
>> to read the signs you have inscribed
>> in history and in the cosmos.
> And we pray that you will not let us fall
>> into fear and faint-heartedness.
> Because your oceans are so immense,
>> and our boats are so small and fragile.

In the fraternity of Lamsai, a name meaning in the Thai language *Garden of peace and celestial beauty*, the Minister was able to see for himself how the friars in accordance with the mandate of the last Pentecost Chapter sought to combine contemplation with a presence among the poor. Situated near the great and noisy city of Bangkok, their house is a place of welcome and of spiritual and bodily care for numerous victims of AIDS. Moreover the members of this international fraternity joyfully imparted to him the news that, with the help of God and of the Seraphic Father, they would soon be welcoming the first candidates to the year of probation. The Minister in his turn gave thanks to the Lord who was now in his providence granting to the tender little plant of the Thailand project, after innumerable trials and sufferings, some growth and hope for the future.

Thereafter the Minister journeyed to Udon Thani in the northeast of the country for a fraternal meeting with the ministers and friars who had assembled there from all parts of the vast continent as well as from some of the more remote islands, such as Bismarck, Solomon, and Tonga. All were given lodging in the house of the bishop of that place. Its magnificent garden was lush with rhododendron, eucalyptus, and myrtle bushes, with delicate orchids and wild magnolias, but was also, alas, home to some snakes.

For three days the friars talked among themselves about the signs of hope and of sorrow which they noticed in their provinces and fraternities. All were convinced that in the future the Order would have to present a more Asiatic face if the universal brotherhood is to be transformed into an instrument of peace and of evangelization, increasingly catholic and apostolic but at the same time ever more ecumenical and ecological. The friars of Asia and Oceania promised that even in their poverty they would come to the assistance of other provinces and of the numerous international projects of the Order.

In these lands and on these seas the Chinese Year of the Butterfly was just beginning. A bright day in the month of February was dedicated to an experience of inculturation. For this purpose the friars who had come from Rome, Papua, and all the other quarters set out on a journey towards the border with Laos. They first made a stop at a place called Wat Phra That Bang Phuan in order to make a fraternal visit to a venerable Buddhist monastery. After they had spent some time in the shrine, a saffron-robed monk offered on his own accord to predict the future for the Minister. And so, according to the custom of the place, the Minister, reclining with the other friars on a bamboo mat, had to shake a wooden container rhythmically until there came out of it one of its many hollowed sticks, inside each of which was a minuscule roll of parchment. After the Minister had complied with this ritual under the curious gaze of his companions and of some Buddhist novices, the master read for him the following oracle:

> In this world there are but two elements: beauty and truth.
> Beauty in the heart of the one who loves,
> truth in the arms of the one who tills the land.

The Minister greatly marveled at these words. They seemed to him to be very close to the spirituality of the Poverello of Assisi, who had loved the poor, extolled the beauty of the universe in song, and asked his brothers to work diligently. While the Minister was thinking how profound these words were and how applicable to the life of his friars, the monk spoke and added the following words:

If you discover how to praise the beauty
   of the world in song,
even in the most solitary desert place
   you will find a hearing.

Pondering all that he had heard, the Minister understood as never before that his brotherhood, scattered throughout the world in many places amid war, poverty, and conflict was living out the destiny of those who sow in tears; at the same time it hoped one day to reap a harvest in joy and exultation.

That same day the friars also visited Phuttamamakasamak-kom, a place famous for its amazing collection of statues and monuments representing the various types of Buddha, Vishnu, and Siva. Thus they consciously implemented the mandate of their Constitutions, according to which all should "discern the seeds of the Word of God and his mysterious presence in the world of today and also in many aspects of other religions and cultures" (93.2). Towards evening they boarded a rickety boat and were taken on an excursion along the Mekong River which, in the region of Nongh Khai, marks the boundary between Thailand and mysterious Laos. Seated on the deck of the boat and having consumed a delicious supper whose main ingredient was fish, they gave themselves up to silent contemplation of the beauty of the star-studded horizon. At a certain point they all found themselves listening in silence to the Tao, the wisdom innate in all creation. They heard it in the mild evening breeze and in the sweet music which came wafting towards them from both banks of the river, as well as in the moving melody of the setting of the sun and in the soundless music of the spheres. These are the words which the Minister heard that evening:

With dampened clay are formed the pots,
   but only their hollowness allows jugs to be filled.
From wood are constructed doors and windows,
   but only the empty space they create
   makes the house habitable.

What is seen is indeed useful,
   but what is essential remains invisible.
You possess only what you give away,
   because what you try to keep will be lost to you.

That night everyone understood how the brotherhood, wherever it finds itself, can contribute to evangelization and to the future of the world only if it adopts an attitude of profound listening, of minority, of solidarity with the poor, and of respectful dialogue with all religions and cultures.

During a farewell ceremony held in the house of the bishop of Udon Thani, the friars prayed together in the words of an ancient mystic of the Buddhist tradition:

May the rain of burning coals and of stones
   and the rain of weapons
   become a rain of flowers.
May the poor, benumbed by cold,
   find warmth and compassion
   and may coolness come to all who are exposed to
   scorching heat.
May the sick find healing
   and may an end come to all the violence in the world.
May the fearful live in peace
   and may the oppressed find liberation and justice.
May prisoners discover a new way of life
   and may all who are sorrowful find courage and hope.
May the disinherited possess the earth
   and may all live in friendship and respect.
For the only wealth that always grows bigger
   when it is given away with both hands
   is love and peace.

Thereupon all returned spiritually strengthened and inwardly enlightened to their own provinces and fraternities scattered throughout Asia and the immense Pacific Ocean as the Minister made his way back to Rome, back to the hill fragrant with the sweet scent of jasmine.

Udon Thanai, February 8, 1993

33. Concerning the beginning of the year of St. Clare in Africa

Background: In August 1993 the Minister General together with Peter Williams visited Kenya and Uganda. The occasion was a Chapter of Mats in Nairobi, with participants also from Tanzania, Malawi, Rwanda, Burundi, Uganda, Zambia, and Madagascar. In the monastery of the Poor Clares in Mbarara (Uganda), on the feast of St. Clare (11 August), they celebrated the beginning of the Jubilee Year of St. Clare (1993-1994).

In the month of August 1993, as the Order of the Lesser Brothers was commemorating the first ten years of its new Africa Project and also when eight hundred years had passed since the birth of St. Clare, Brother Hermann once more left his jasmine-scented hill in Rome and, having sought the consent of the other Ministers General and of the Abbess of the Proto-monastery of St. Clare to spend the feast of St. Clare in Africa, set out with Brother Peter for Kenya and Uganda.

In Nairobi all the brothers of the Vice-Province of St. Francis were awaiting their arrival in order to recount to them something of their experiences, needs, and hopes. The young brothers of that continent said to him: "Do not come bringing a full pitcher. Come rather with an empty calabash. We will show you how to fill it." And as he saw the numerous young brothers of all tribes and nations who wanted to join the brotherhood in these days, he was reminded of the saying of Scripture: "Thus says the Lord of hosts: In those days ten men from nations of every language shall take hold of a Jew, grasping his garment and saying, 'Let us go with you, for we have heard that God is with you'" (Zec 8:23). Brother Ayele from Kenya sat one evening with Brother Hermann from Rome on a straw mat and drank tea with him. Ayele said: "You are sitting with me on the same level. In Africa that is usually not so. Our chiefs are accustomed to sit higher than the ordinary people. I love my people but I am also happy to be your younger brother who sits with you on the same level."

Brother Hermann spoke to them as they were all assembled about the oneness of Africa with the worldwide brotherhood and what in his opinion evangelization means: "To build a ship does not mean to weave the sails, to cast the nails, to shape the wood as a carpenter, to read the heavenly signs, but rather to waken in all those who intend to sail in her the longing for the open sea" (Exupéry). Only by a longing for God in contemplation, Brother

Hermann added, can the brotherhood and the whole Franciscan family initiate a new evangelization. Brother Expositus from Tanzania called out to him a proverb from the tribe of the Xeruba: "The peace at the hearth of your hut outweighs the enmity of the entire world."

This gave the Minister the occasion to say in reply that indeed in the Order of the Lesser Brothers it is not a matter of writing ever new learned manifestos urging inculturation or contemplation, directing lengthy appeals for peace to the whole world. More important is beginning with oneself, using quite small steps—to close doors quietly, to remember the name of a brother or sister, to avoid treading a flower needlessly underfoot, to learn respectful silence and at the same time to speak foreign languages, to show mercy and at the same time to be able to accept it, to know how to plant both rice and roses. During the liturgy at the conclusion of this Chapter of Mats, he thanked all the friars in the name of the worldwide brotherhood for the implantation of the Order in East Africa and Madagascar. He blessed everyone, white or black, young or old, in the name of Francis and Clare, with these words:

> May the Lord bless your work.
> May your rice fields and banana groves
>   always bear rich fruit.
> May the meat and the milk of your zebus nourish the poor.
> May your doors and your hearts always stand open.
> May your voices and your drums ever
>   praise and glorify the Lord.

Then the Minister continued his journey. He sailed across Lake Victoria to the land of Uganda and after a tedious journey through an area beset by robbers and brigands arrived by way of Entebbe and Kampala and Mbarara in Kashekuro, where the brothers, the bishop, and a crowd of people from the villages of the surrounding savannas awaited him. It was the vigil of the feast of St. Clare, which was at that same moment also being celebrated in Assisi in Umbria with much incense and Gregorian chant and under the presidency of a cardinal of the Holy Roman Church. Here in Kashekuro there was a great gathering of the people with their cattle, to celebrate the Holy Eucharist with the bishop and the Minister while listening to the rhythmic beat of drums and tambourines.

In his homily, which the bishop translated into the language of his people, Brother Hermann compared the Gospel to a brushfire which, having been lit in many places by many brothers of St. Francis and sisters of St. Clare, could one day soon enlighten the whole African continent. He also said that evangelization is what takes place when poor people joyfully recount to one another where fresh water and a plateful of rice and buffalo meat are to be found. It is the task of Christians in Africa, so he continued, to dig many new wells (Gn 26:17-33), to drink from fresh sources, to irrigate thirsty land—including Europe—with water and hope, to watch over the garden of the Church and its basic communities and build on them, to live new visions of a brotherly and sisterly Church, to compose new melodies and sing new songs. He reminded them of the saying of the ancient Roman poet Ovid that poetry and music only arise from a heart that is at peace with itself. He begged Brother Richard from America, an older brother who led the community, not to leave this place and quoted the African proverb: "When a wise man departs, it is as though a whole library has been destroyed."

At the end of the Mass the bishop was so moved that before the whole assembly he knelt down and humbly begged the Minister General for the blessing of St. Francis and of St. Clare for his diocese, for all its people and all their cattle. And the assembled community was astonished at this gesture and thanked the Lord for this sign of a truly new evangelization.

Late into the night on the grass and between the banana groves around the church of Kashekuro, there arose smoke from great pots of maize, banana, buffalo meat, and millet beer. Far into the darkness of the African night resounded the drums and the hand-clapping of the people.

The solemnity of St. Clare was celebrated by the Lord Bishop and all the brothers from Uganda and Rome with the Poor Ladies in Mbarara. The sisters greeted the Minister in the garden with symbols and words at once African and totally catholic. A young sister with the countenance of the Queen of Sheba offered him a bowl of water, saying: "Here is fresh water to bid you welcome. It is to tell you that we have awaited your visit as parched soil awaits the rain." Brother Hermann drank from the calabash and passed it on to the bishop. A second sister came up and said: "Accept this fruit of our land, a kola nut. I will break it into two, for me to eat one half and you the other. The single kola nut is to tell you that we were already bound to each other before you came." Then the abbess came up and said: "Here is the tabouret (little stool), on which you will sit in our circle not only as our guest but as a part of our family. And we ask you to tell us in the assembly of our family, as is the custom in Africa, about your journey and about our great family." And so it was.

As they all then sat under the great tree, the youngest novice asked him what the Lesser Brothers really understood by evangelization in Africa, a continent with centenary traditions of its own. The Minister answered:

> When we approach another culture, another people, another religion, we must begin by removing our shoes and sandals and remain a long time in silence. For the ground on which we tread is holy ground. If we fail to do this but instead come with our heavy shoes and loud words, we destroy the music and the hopes of the other; even worse, we completely ignore the presence of God who was already there before we came.

He explained that in the past few years brothers have come from all parts of the world to Africa in order to discover there the other half of their souls.

In his homily during the celebration of the Eucharist, Brother Hermann recounted how he had asked his Brother Ministers, the Bishop, and the Abbess of the Proto-monastery in Assisi for permission to be absent from the opening of the Year of St. Clare in Assisi and rather to be present in Africa, for there too St. Clare and her heritage have to be commemorated. All were so overjoyed at hearing this that they clapped their hands, let out loud whoops of joy, and sounded their drums and tambourines. He went on to speak of the three dimensions of contemplation. To begin with, we have to acquire clear eyes and a pure heart in order to recognize the Lord in the Scriptures and in the Holy Eucharist and in the Church. Then it becomes important to have contemplative eyes, open hearts, and open hands for the poor, through whom in a special way the Spirit speaks to the Church and to the family of St. Francis and St. Clare. Finally, contemplation will also transform our relationship with nature and creation since everything created, even though deformed by human hate or human avarice, is a sign of and a word from the Creator.

Following the mind of the little Brother of Assisi, he encouraged the sisters of St. Clare in Africa also to evangelize tired old Europe by their example.

Be patient in affliction, wakeful in prayer, persevering in your work, cheerful and happy in your dealings with the poor, grateful for all blessings, tireless in your gratitude to the Lord of History. Have faith in the creative power of contemplation. For it is not flight from the world. It is the power with which all religions, together and with the help of God, will create a new, more just, more peaceful world.

He ended by passing on to the sisters in Uganda the blessing which he had himself received in Kenya: "Let the peace at the hearth of your home outweigh the enmity of the entire world."

After they had fortified themselves in the monastery garden of the Poor Ladies with a frugal meal, the Minister of this brotherhood traveled back to Rome, crossing Lake Victoria, the waters of Aswan, the Gulf of Arabia, and the Gulf of Naples, to pass some time again on his Jasmine Hill and to reflect on all those things which the sisters and brothers in Africa had taught him, both for his own benefit and for the edification of the Franciscan and Clarian family throughout the world.

Kampala, August 13, 1993

1994

34. Concerning an encounter of the Minister with the South Pacific

Background: On his journey to Papua New Guinea at the beginning of 1994, the Minister General first visited the brothers in Pakistan, Singapore, and Indonesia.

The wisdom of the Sufis

At the beginning of the year 1994 (in China it was the Year of the Dog), Brother Hermann set out on a journey to the Pacific Ocean to make the acquaintance of the brothers and sisters in distant Papua, New Guinea. On the way he stopped a few days in Karachi and Lahore, cities of Pakistan, which unfortunately he had never visited. The brothers were preparing to celebrate their chapter, and he listened attentively to their proposals, ideas, and experiences in an Islamic context. He was most impressed, as was Brother

Maurice who was accompanying him, by a piece of wisdom handed down from the learned Sufis of the country concerning the "Three Doors" and which was recounted to them by young Brother Yassir from the Punjab.

The Sufis are convinced that you should speak only when your words have passed through three doors. At the first door ask yourself: "Is what I am about to say really true?" If it is, you may proceed to the second door. Once there, ask yourself: "Are the words I am about to utter really necessary?" If this is the case, go to the third door. There ask yourself: "Are my words also friendly?" And so, speak only when your words are at once true, necessary, and friendly.

So the two pilgrims, thoughtful and encouraged, traveled to Singapore, the next stop on their way to Papua.

The Trunk and the Branches

In Singapore the two visitors were amazed, not so much by the tropical vegetation and the Crocodile Park which can be visited there as by the growing number of young men of many languages and cultures who have entered the Order over the years from Malaysia, Sarawak, Brunei, Sri Lanka, and Singapore. For this they thanked the Lord of History, who in his loving kindness brings it about that in the great book of the Franciscan family new pages are constantly being turned and that on the venerable trunk of our brotherhood new branches are constantly growing. In a conversation with all the members of this new custody, the Minister spoke of the realistic utopia of a family, united though diverse in language and color of the skin, which is entering upon a new age. As he took his leave, he reminded them of something said by Leonardo da Vinci: "When people are traveling together in the same boat, then neither the color of the skin, nor the age, nor the religion and culture of the passengers are what counts. Nor is the past of any account. What counts is to surmount together the storms, to arrive together in safety and together to discover new horizons."

So the two pilgrims continued their journey, making the third stop on their way to Papua, this time in Indonesia.

The Magic of a Surname

In this land, made up of countless islands, they were once more surprised by the great number of young friars. This time the brothers came from Java, Timor, Flores, Bali, from the lesser and greater Sonda islands, from the Moluccas, Sulawesi, and Irian Jaya. At Pagal on Flores during the welcoming ceremony, the Minister received as a greeting gift a live chicken, which at once crowed its salutation, as well as beer made from bananas and rice. On being asked by the brothers about his own origin, Brother Hermann told how he too was born in rural parts but that in his own home area of Westphalia there did not grow rice, mango, coffee, and cocoa but only potatoes, cabbage, carrots, and a few poor apples. In Irian Jaya a certain Brother Saul accepted him into his own mountain tribe of the "Halu." By way of explanation he declared: "I cannot pro–nounce your exotic family name but it contains the name of our tribe (scHALUck). Therefore you now belong to us."

In the chapter of the Poor Sisters of St. Clare in Pacet on Java, ten of the brothers of the Province made profession of solemn vows into the hands of the Minister from Rome. In his homily Brother Hermann said, among other things: "The Kingdom of Heaven is like an international fraternity with its members drawn from the most diverse lands: Ivan is from Smolensk in Russia, Georges is from Normandy, Halim is from Syria, Henry from Milwaukee, Carlos from Arequipa in Peru, Georges from Africa, and Aloysius from Java. Three are priests, four are laymen, all are brothers. They are living the peace which they proclaim to others in their own hearts and in their own house. For in the Kingdom of God it is of no importance whether one is black or white or yellow, Polynesian or European, professor or campesino, cleric or lay. All are brothers and sisters under the one Lord, whose kindness rains like the tropical monsoon on everyone without distinction." He invited the brothers of Indonesia to prepare themselves for a new mission of the Order in China. And so our pilgrims arrived at last in Aitape in Papua New Guinea.

The Mother of Wise Thoughts

The Minister's first action in these regions of the South Pacific was to visit the Poor Ladies of St. Clare and celebrate the Eucharist with them. Then just as St. Francis once asked St. Clare for spiritual counsel, he begged them for some instruction on contemplation. They answered him with words from one of the Desert Fathers, Diadochus of Photike: "If the door of the steamroom remains open, the heat will quickly escape. Just so in a man who is a chatterbox; any mindfulness of God disappears through the door of his mouth . . . precious ideas ever avoid a torrent of words since they shy away from hubbub and feverish phantasies. So silence at the right time is precious, for it is the mother of wise thoughts."

Having partaken of a frugal meal, the Minister and the brothers drove to the capital, Port Moresby. There the brothers dedicate themselves to the cultivation of orchids and lotus flowers; from the sale of these they cover their subsistence. So our visitors came to know first of all the white lotus from Egypt *(Nymphaea alba)*, which in the land of the Nile is to this day a symbol of birth and rebirth, flowering from April to November. Even more familiar became the Oriental lotus *(Nuphar lutea)*, smaller than its Egyptian cousin and in contrast to it yellow in color. It is the symbol of purity and the spiritual flowering which comes from the depths of the human heart. Finally they admired the Indian lotus *(Nymphaea rosea)* on which, according to a Brahmin tradition, the Creator God Prajapati glides softly over the waters. In the novitiate house in Port Moresby the Minister had the happiness of clothing in the habit of probation five candidates from the most diverse tribes of Melanesia. All thanked the Lord also for this new branch on the tree of the fraternity, and all sang the psalm in which the numerous distant isles are called upon to rejoice in the Lord and his goodness (Ps 97).

Isles, Arks, and Boats

To conclude their visit to the South Pacific, Brother Timothy from Aitape had promised the visitors that he would take them by boat to two small islands lying off the coast. There in the last century missionaries from distant Germany had begun the evangelization of Papuasia. After a tranquil crossing, the visitors greeted the children and the elders of the village, heard an account of the fishing and of the building of a new church, and listened to Latin and German Christmas songs which had been handed down to the present day. After they had been refreshed with some coconut milk, they set out on their return journey to Aitape. While the motorboat sped like an arrow over the waves, the Minister reflected on all that he had seen and heard on his long journey as well as on the many difficult problems and challenges facing his Order in the world and in Rome. It came to his mind that it was important on the threshold of a new age to be not mere administrators of the inheritance of the past but also precursors and pioneers for the generations of the future; that in accordance with the so-called "Noah principle" it was for the brothers not so much a matter of being able to forecast the weather as of building in good time secure arks and safe boats; that the Franciscan family is like a great delta, fed by a single source and opening into a single ocean; that the great ocean is made up of billions of tiny drops; that, as has been said by a spiritual master of our time, only one who has had dreams and visions can begin a movement. And as the sun went down behind the mangrove forests of Papua and the gentle waves of the Pacific sang their friendly song, our passenger from Rome fell quietly into a soft sleep.

The awakening a short time later, however, was anything but soft. Brother Timothy, experienced sailor and vicar general of the Aitape Diocese, missed in the half-darkness the entrance into the mouth of the river and ran the boat aground. A wave washed out into the wide ocean not only the Minister's gentle dreams but also some Roman decrees and ordinances which he always carried with him. He swam and waded to the land nearby and sat down on a tree trunk, itself previously washed ashore, in order to reflect on his situation, allowing the water of the ocean to drip from him and observing the recovery of the boat which was being aided by some friendly men from the nearby fishing village. They then returned to the fraternity.

When all his clothing had been dried and he had taken his leave of the brothers and sisters in hospitable Papuasia, the Minister, enriched by many new experiences, finally journeyed back to Rome, to the hill redolent of the scent of wild jasmine.

Port Moresby, February 2, 1994

35. Concerning a pilgrimage to Our Lady of Luján

Background: This story is based on a journey to visit the three Franciscan provinces in Argentina in April 1994. Important parts of the journey included taking part in a biennial meeting of all the ministers provincial of the subcontinent, visiting houses of formation and traveling to a mission station on the border with Bolivia.

The Memory of the Future

It was a day in spring when, having attended the African Synod in the Vatican as one of the few whites, Brother Hermann set off in the direction of Argentina, where he was to take part in a meeting of all the ministers and custodes of the South American subcontinent. The encounter took place in the shadow of the cathedral dedicated to Our Lady of Luján, in the southern section of Buenos Aires.

There in the spirit of the Rule—according to which each must make known to the other his own needs and hopes—the talk was about the formation of the brothers, the option for the poor, the commitment of the Franciscan family to peace, justice, and creation. But it was also about the participation of the provinces of the subcontinent in the projects of the other continents and of the entire Order.

In the presence of the ministers and delegates, Brother Hermann spoke of hope as "the memory of the future" and urged them on as follows: "Your fraternities are like the boats traveling on the Rio Grande, the Orinoco, the Amazon, and the Rio de la Plata. Don't ever stop rowing! Because as soon as you rest the oars on the boat, you will be borne backwards."

He also quoted for them a maxim which he had heard in Asia where he had been a short time before: "Always keep your face turned to the sun; in this way the shadows fall a long way behind you."

Story of the Sun and of the Inquiring Novice

He spoke in this way to the brothers, confirming them in their commitment in the service of freedom, reconciliation, and peace. After that the Minister who had come from Rome made his way to the Luis Bolaños Institute, where the young brothers of all three provinces of the country are being taught philosophy, theology, and the spirituality of St. Francis.

Together with their professors, both clerical and lay, male and female, the students were assembled in the Great Hall to hear the admonitions of the Minister and the replies to their questions. First of all they asked him what he could tell them about the theme of contemplation. And he began to tell them a story taken from the monastic tradition of the Nubian desert, a story which he had been told during the synod by a bishop from Eritrea.

Once upon a time there was a novice who wanted to become a saint and to see the Lord. He asked his confreres what he should do to attain this noble goal; all of them recommended fasting, prayer, vigils, manual labor, and still more prayer.

For some years the novice worked hard at all of this but he noticed that no change had taken place in his life and that he was not seeing the Lord. Disconsolate, he then went to the abbot, lamenting that he was not being successful in becoming a saint and was no closer to seeing God. The abbot replied: "You cannot make yourself a saint on your own. It is like sunrise in the morning. Is there anything you can do to make the sun rise?" The novice sadly agreed: "Nothing."

After a long silence the novice asked the abbot: "But if things are so, that I cannot of myself become a saint, why then does the Rule impose fasting, vigils, penitential exercises, and hard work?" Then the abbot looked smilingly at the young brother and said: "All this is necessary so that in the morning when the sun finally makes it appearance you may be awake and its first rays can fall on your face."

And Brother Hermann reminded himself and all the brothers of the words of warning sprayed by an unknown artist on the walls of the Roman curia of the Lesser Brothers: "No one can prevent the sun from rising each morning."

The Story of the Flies and the Lukewarm Religious

Then a novice from Catamarca asked what is to be understood by the "universality of the Order" and the "solidarity of individuals with the whole." In his explanation the Minister made use of a simile. Our fraternity is like an orchestra which is performing a cantata of J. S. Bach. There are very different instruments: violins, flutes, drums, trumpets, cymbals, violas, and many others. There are different rhythms in the cantata and different tempos such as *allegro, andante, dolce, con fuoco*. There are singers and instrumentalists, soloists and members of the choir. All the instruments and all the singers are important; no one must be missing. Each one does something different but all contribute to the overall harmony. The piece can be successful only if all listen to each other and if, in addition, they do not lose sight of the conductor.

To the question as to why some brothers enthusiastically embrace the way of life of the Poor Man of Assisi and later leave the brotherhood, Brother Hermann answered again with a story coming this time from the Egyptian desert which he had visited the previous year. In the life of fraternity things happen the way they do when a dog is let loose to follow a rabbit. The dog gives chase and barks its heart out. But many other dogs join in the attack and all chase the rabbit. But then the moment arrives when all those dogs who, not having seen the rabbit, since it is always ahead of them, grow tired and so some of them give up the chase. On the other hand those who have sight of the rabbit keep going to the very end. Then he rounded off this story with the lesson which the Desert Fathers and Mothers of the Coptic rite had already derived from it: "Only those who through contemplation keep their eyes fixed on Jesus can endure to the end.

He then added another saying, this one of African origin: "Flies keep their distance from a boiling kettle but they alight on one that is lukewarm." So it is that although demons flee from a brother who burns with the fire of the Spirit, they torment the one who is lukewarm.

New Evangelization and a New Song

When another brother asked him what the Saint of Assisi meant by evangelization, Brother Hermann began to give an account of the work of the brothers in Syria, Israel, and Jordan; he spoke of his visit to Haj Ismail Jaber, the commander of the PLO at Jericho in Palestine, a visit he made with the Custos of the Holy Land. He told them of the martyrdom of the brothers in Bosnia and in Rwanda and of the witness of the brothers in far-off Kazakhstan. What is important, he concluded, is to replace evil with good. In a situation of conflict, one should take the first step towards reconciliation. In every situation one should try to be free and cleansed of all interior feelings of hate and rivalry in order to follow the footprints of Christ crucified amidst all cultures, in an unbiased and benevolent manner. By way of conclusion the Minister announced that he would be going on the following day to Pichanal, in the north of the country, to hand over to Chucuri, tribal chief of the Guaranì, a large plot of land which had belonged to the Order. Two hundred families could then cultivate it and live there.

But when another brother still wished to know why we speak today about a "new" evangelization, the Minister replied in the words of Augustine of Hippo: "A new song does not suit an old man. Only new men can learn a new song, that is, those who have been renewed from within and have been purified by the grace of God and already belong to the new covenant and the Kingdom of the Spirit who renews the earth. Our whole life belongs to the new Kingdom so that if we are to sing about this Kingdom, we need new songs. Therefore, sing new songs, not just with the tongue, but with your whole life" (*On the Psalms*).

Concluding Prayer

At the conclusion of the meeting Brother Hermann was joined by many brothers of his Order and a large crowd of people in celebrating a solemn Eucharist in the basilica of Luján. When the young brothers sang many new songs, the congregation was greatly amazed. Afterwards they recited together this prayer:

Lord, grant that we may become in our Church the living gifts of your Spirit. We have need of brothers and sisters who know how to listen, who create peace, who by their example give direction. We have need of brothers and sisters who instill courage, who give witness, and who tell the truth without being hurtful. We have need of brothers and sisters, young and old, who keep themselves anchored in you and who because of this radiate hope.

Bestow on us, Lord, the grace to be ever persevering in prayer and to see that our prayer also becomes action. Grant, O Lord, that through the intercession of Mary, Mother of the poor, we may become a missionary brotherhood which serves the poor and the persecuted and which believes in its future.

After all departed the Minister returned to Rome to his hill which was fragrant with jasmine and a light scent of wild roses.

Buenos Aires, May 2, 1994

Chapter 6
1995-1996

1995

36. A visit by the Minister to the Golden Horn

Background: In March 1995 the Minister General and Tecle Vetrali (Venice Province) visited the Ecumenical Patriarch at the Phanar (Istanbul) and a church served by friars of the Tuscany Province.

"There are many colors but only a single rainbow."

Spring in the Bosphorus

It was spring again. The Muslim world had begun Ramadan and Christians were preparing to celebrate the season of Lent in 1995. On the fragrantly scented hill of jasmine of the Roman curia, there came to fruition the plan for an "ecumenical gesture" on the Bosphorus, in the country of the Fathers of Cappadocia, who were distinguished for their courageous faith and powerful word, where East and West still meet. For some months with a tenacious gentleness, the Minister had been requesting an audience with His Holiness, Patriarch Bartholomew. It was Brother Hermann's firm belief that the Catholic tradition does not lie in tending the ashes but in taking good care that the fire of hope is not extinguished. At the airport of Istanbul, the Minister and his companion, Brother Tecle, were welcomed by a certain monk named Gennadios, who with exquisite courtesy accompanied his guests to their hotel. That evening he brought them to a seashore restaurant specializing in fish, where the scent of lavender and rosemary was heralding the arrival of spring.

The Audience

With the monk Gennadios as their guide, the two Romans visited the principal monuments of the city on the following morning, which was a Saturday. First called "Rome of the East" and later Byzantium, Constantinople was conquered in 1453 by the

Turks. According to a very ancient tradition, this city is the repository of the relics of the Apostle Andrew and the apostle's disciples, Luke and Timothy. Continuing their tour, the visitors arrived at the *Chora*, a church which the Emperor Theodosius (504-595) had erected. Afterwards, they came to *Hagia Sophia* (Church of Divine Wisdom) where since 1453 it has not been possible to celebrate the Divine Liturgy. Then they visited the Blue Mosque. It was about midday when they eventually reached Phanar Hill and St. George Church, which since 1612 has been the residence of the Ecumenical Patriarch of the East. His Holiness received his Roman guests with exquisite kindness and conversed with them alternately in Italian and German. He recalled the Councils of Chalcedon and Nicaea, the fall of the city in 1453 and the need for communion between the Churches of the East and West. He expressed his joy that he would soon visit Rome to give the fraternal embrace of the Apostle Andrew to the Apostle Peter.

As a sign and confirmation that the friars throughout the whole world support this desire, Brother Hermann presented him with a replica of the San Damiano Cross. The Patriarch kissed it reverently and gave it a place of honor in his own study. In exchange he presented his guests with a glass-mounted seal of the Ecumenical Patriarch. Furthermore he invited them, together with some other members of the Holy Synod, to a frugal meal which they shared with hearts full of joy.

In the afternoon the monk Gennadios accompanied his guests on a trip to the island of Chalki in the Bosphorus and to a monastery there which can be reached only in a horse-drawn carriage. They paid a visit to the library and saw more precious items. A young monk named Jeremiah from Mount Athos gave the Minister a jewel case of aromatic incense, the Eastern scents of which would be blended shortly afterwards—*"non commixtionem passus, neque divisionem"* (unchanged, not separated)—with the fragrant perfume of Roman incense and jasmine. And while the skies above Istanbul were resounding with many voices proclaiming "Allah akbar" (God is great), the visitors returned to their hotel.

The Large and Small Throne

On Sunday morning our visitors returned to Phanar Hill. They were invited to participate with the Patriarch in the liturgy according to the Greek Orthodox Rite. In preparation they had already meditated from early morning on the words of Origen:

"Seek to drink from the spring of the Spirit which is already in you. In the depths of your being is the fountain of living water from which the inexhaustible rivers of spiritual feeling gush forth, unless they are blocked by earth and stones. But hasten to clear the rubble, that is, to rid yourself of sloth and defilement of heart" (*Homilies on Genesis*, SCh 7 bis, p. 307).

An Eastern tradition called for the setting up in St. George Church of a large throne for His Holiness. The Patriarch himself conferred an unexpected honor on the Minister from Rome, by seating him opposite himself on a small lower throne. Inwardly moved, Brother Hermann prayed for himself and for all his brothers and sisters, not with the words of the Fathers or Mothers of the Western Church but as Brother Francis inspired him at that moment:

> Let us be satisfied with humble places. Grant us to serve without arrogance or vanity. Make us at home with the earth, with the poor and humble. Teach us how to wait, to listen and to remain silent. Make us small and weak, in such a way that others may even be able to come to our assistance. Give us that most beautiful of all privileges: not to have any privilege. Send us forth from here on the highways of the world to seek your name in all religions, confessions, and creatures.

And while the choir of monks raised their voices in chant, the words of Hildegard of Bingen came to mind: "Singing softens hard hearts. It gives rise to tears of compunction and summons the Holy Spirit." The whole assembly was enveloped in the enticing aroma of eastern incense. At the dismissal, all together sang a chant taken from a hymn by Ephrem of Nisibis:

> In your goodness make me worthy to find grace before you in paradise. You are the treasure which contains all perfumes, the source of all scents. The breath of your scent assuages my thirst. You are a perfume nourishing all creatures of every age. Whoever breathes you will be filled with eternal joy and will not be content any more with the bread of earth. Jesus Christ has called us to the banquet of his eternal kingdom in paradise" (*Hymn to Paradise*, SCh 137, p. 151).

Farewell

Finally our pilgrims paid a visit to the church of Santa Maria in Draperis, where some friars from Tuscany have a ministry. The conversation was about the mission of the Lesser Brothers and of Franciscan sisters to foster friendly relations with Islam and with the other religions and confessions. Questions were asked as to how their presence in Turkey could be revived through new incentives. The Minister proposed the setting up in their house of an embassy or a consulate from the entire Franciscan family to the Ecumenical Patriarch.

Just before they left the Golden Horn behind them and boarded the plane to travel from East to West, they heard for the last time the slow call of the muezzin announcing the three days of *bairan*, the joyful conclusion of Ramadan. For Latin Christians on the other hand as well as for the brothers on the Jasmine Hill, the season of Lent would soon begin. This year the maxim of John Climacus was chosen as a leitmotif for Lent at the curia of the Lesser Brothers: "The love of the one and triune God is manifested in the love between brothers and sisters."

Istanbul, March 5, 1995

37. A meeting of the friars in Malta

Background: The Plenary Council of the Order of Friars Minor was held in Malta in May 1995. The main agenda topic was reviewing the Ratio Evangelisationis, *a document called for by the 1991 general chapter for presentation to the 1997 general chapter.*

"The smallest islands have the widest horizons."

Shipwrecks and Snakes

It was the beautiful month of May in the year 1995 when, at the invitation of the Minister General, fifty brothers from all over the world landed on the island of Malta for the Plenary Council of the Order.

They were longing to come to grips with the difficult theme of evangelization in order to prepare themselves for the next general chapter. The venue for the meeting in Malta was the Portiuncula, a retreat house managed by the friars of the island. From its elevated position it commands a sweeping view of the sea. Since there was not room for everyone at the Portiuncula, some friars were housed further inland with the Jesuits.

As the brothers soon discovered, Malta is an island located on the dividing line between Europe and Africa. It covers a small amount of territory but has a rich history. In one of its rocky bays Paul, the Apostle of the Gentiles, came ashore after he was shipwrecked while on a voyage to Rome. When he was nearly on the point of death after having been bitten by a snake, he was given welcome hospitality for three months by a certain Publius. Paul converted many people to the Lord (Acts 27-28).

This jewel of the Mediterranean was later conquered by the Arabs, visited by Norman Crusaders, and donated by the Emperor Charles V to the Knights of St. John, who in 1565 successfully defended it from an assault by the Turks under the leadership of Suleyman the Magnificent. Thus did it come to pass that the sons of St. Francis were also able to set foot on the island.

The Smiling Madonna

At the opening of the Plenary Council in the Sanctuary of the Madonna of Mellieha, the Minister General preached on the following theme: St. Francis was one captivated by a longing for the open sea and its wide horizons. He had always experienced an intense desire to travel overseas, to cross the Mediterranean, to go beyond Europe, to reach Syria and the Holy Land (LM 9:5), to meet the sultan of Egypt (1Cel 55-56).

The Minister said that the brotherhood in no way needed new and verbose documents but rather fresh incentives springing from the Gospel, vivid examples of a living hope. To be able to move toward new shores, toward the new millennium, there is need primarily of brothers and sisters who will be solidly anchored both in contemplation and in love of the poor. The brotherhood this time chose Malta for its discussions for two reasons: because they wished to be inspired by the example of Paul, who despite the shipwreck did not allow himself to be discouraged, and because often the small islands display the widest horizons.

The Minister thanked everyone for coming and in conclusion invoked on their labors the patronage of the Madonna of Mellieha. Since it was a time when elsewhere in the Mediterranean Basin statues of the Madonna were shedding bitter tears, Brother Hermann implored the Madonna of Malta to bestow a friendly smile on the brothers and on the whole Franciscan family. Then the friars got down to work.

Hope is the Memory of the Future

In those days the sky of the young summer stretched like silk over the hill of the Portiuncula, over the rocky shore and crystalline sea, over the dusty hills and stony fields. The murmur of the waves and the hot wind, together with the chirping of the cicadas, provided nature's music for the brothers as they prayed and sang and studied the documents, discussing them in small groups as well as in plenary sessions.

It was the Minister's warning and prayer to all the friars that they would begin the announcement of the Gospel in contemplation and that they would always come back to this: "Let us make this possible: that we transmit only what we have personally heard, seen, and tasted." He reminded them also that in its journey toward the new millennium the brotherhood has need of dreams and visions. In fact, the dreams are like the stars. The navigator and voyager of the night cannot reach them, but from them travelers can get their true bearings.

Brother Hermann invited all to experience a "mysticism of open eyes," on the model which Francis used. And in their new *Ratio Evangelisationis*, to be promulgated at Pentecost in 1996, the friars wrote:

> We see many shadows in our world, in our history, in our Church and in our Order, but we also see many lights. We are conscious of our deep concerns but the hope we keep alive is deeper still. We see countless colors but recognize that they make up a single light.
>
> In their cultures, languages and religions, people are like large stones—countless, multicolored and different from each other. All together, however, they form one single mosaic in the sight of God.
>
> At the same time we give thanks to God, Lord of our history, for the bright times and for the dark times of our brotherhood. And to all we wish to announce peace, "to those far away and to those nearby" (Is 57:19).
>
> We acknowledge that this is our vocation: to protect life, to share bread with the poor and to break each day the Bread

by which the Lord of our history comes to us. In the sorrows and wounds of today's world, we wish to behold the sorrow of our Lord Jesus Christ. And, in the company of the many sisters and brothers everywhere along the way, we will celebrate his Resurrection wherever wars will have come to an end, the poor shall have been set free and comfort given to the sorrowful.

The Smile of God on All Creation

At the end of those days in Malta, there was a concert at the Portiuncula—a choir, a lady soloist, a harp, a harpsichord, and a lyre. The intention was to bear witness to the friars that the word of redemption and freedom speaks—and certainly not as a final measure—the language of art and music. As has been demonstrated by the great mystics of the whole world and not only of Europe, salvation which comes from God should be not just visible but audible as well.

Hildegard of Bingen, a German region on the Rhine, once said:

Sweetly echoes the magnificent sound of the living elements, just like the harmonious voice of the human spirit. Every element has its own special sound from God but all together they resonate like the single note of the zither and other stringed instruments when played in perfect harmony.

The concert audience listened in total silence and attention. In expressing everyone's thanks to all the singers and instrumentalists, the Minister General quoted a thought from J. S. Bach: "Music is God's smile on all creation." This phrase will also find a fitting place in the *Ratio Evangelisationis*.

In the neolithic Temple of Hagar Qim, which predates the Pyramid of Ghiza, the brothers who had come from all over the world shared a final contemplative experience. Mindful of the fact that traces and seeds of salvation are present in all ages, they prayerfully recited there Brother Francis's *Canticle of the Creatures*.

They concluded with the following intercessions:

Lord, give us vast horizons, a profound hope and a clear sense of direction on our journey into the future. We are traveling together through the universe like passengers in a little boat, watching a reliable star to guide us. Our life depends on goods that are limited and perishable. It is the task of each one of us in the boat to do all we can for peace and justice. Against annihilation we can defend ourselves only if we are attentive to and of mutual service to each other. Our future depends on the love and care with which we treat you, your creation, our little boat and one another.

By Air and Sea

At the moment of departure, the Minister gave to all the participants, in addition to the greeting of peace, a pebble picked by him in the place where St. Paul had involuntarily come ashore. And while on the horizon twelve white sails crisscrossed in the Bay of St. Paul, and the soft waves of the *mare magnum* skipped among the reefs and rocks as they have done for millennia, the friars who had come from all parts of the world gathered their baggage, took with them the pebble, and departed, some by way of water, some by way of air, towards their provinces and custodies.

The Minister with his companions returned to his Roman hill which was scented with woodland jasmine, thyme, and sweet almonds.

Bahar-Ic-Caghac, May 21, 1995

38. On a pilgrimage to Santiago de Compostela

Background: In the fall of 1995, two large meetings were held in Santiago de Compostela, Spain. The first brought together two young friars from each province and the second one included all the ministers provincial of Europe. The Minister General's book referred to here is the German edition of these Fioretti.

"How beautiful upon the mountains are the feet of the messenger who announces peace, who brings good news" (Is 52:7).

"If you think you are standing, watch out that you do not fall" (1Cor 10:12)

October had already come upon us and it was not long after the solemn festival of our Seraphic Father Francis. At the Portiuncula the Minister General was bidding welcome to brothers from all over the world whose task was the formation of postulants and preparation for their year of novitiate. He had said to them that despite all the difficulties they should pursue their journey with courage and lead the candidates whom the Lord still gives us to take their first steps in the Order. Then he left in haste for Santiago de Compostela to meet the ministers gathered there from all over Europe, to celebrate with them the Eucharist on the tomb of the Apostle James and to encourage them to find new ways to tell the people about the Gospel, from Cape Finisterre to the Urals and from the North Pole to the Cape of Good Hope. During the early afternoon of the twelfth day of October, after a short time given to exercising brother body amid the apple and olive trees of Galicia, he bathed. By some mishap he lost his footing on the watery floor and broke his right leg.

And so it happened that instead of flying the next day as he had planned to the Middle East, to Syria, Jordan, and Lebanon, he was granted the unexpected grace of leading and directing all the brothers of the world from an unusual position for him—not from the noble Jasmine Hill in Rome or from a fast jet plane above the clouds, not by means of letters or other writings, and not even as a pilgrim traveling to the very ends of the earth to visit the brothers and sisters. It was rather that he viewed the world in silence and contemplation from a hospital bed in La Rosaleda Policlinic in the city of the Apostle James. It was then that he found himself much closer to Mother Earth whose colors he had but a few months earlier described in a book. Unexpectedly and not by choice, but in truth to his benefit, he became aware that after traveling hurriedly through numerous continents, his present situation offered him the opportunity of experiencing in a real and personal way the beauty of solitude and tranquil contemplation. He found himself reflecting on the profound truth of the ancient Roman saying: "The Via Appia is less tiring and hazardous for those who are not traveling in a hurry." There came to his mind too the word of holy Scripture: "If you think you are standing, watch out that you do not fall" (1Cor 10:12).

"That which fills your heart with joy sets your feet dancing."

As he thus lay on his sickbed with pain as a constant companion, he recalled that on the day when he broke his leg his address to the European ministers provincial assembled in Santiago had been uplifting but at the same time sobering since he had urged them to take quick and effective steps in the area of evangelization and implanting the Order in various parts of the world. He recalled too how in his homily he had eagerly said to them: "How beautiful upon the mountains are the feet of the messenger who announces peace, who brings good news . . ." to different cultures and continents (Is 52:7). A month before while in Santiago on another pilgrimage, the Minister had quoted to the young brothers from all over the world an African proverb, applying it to the journey towards the new millennium: "That which fills your heart with joy sets your feet dancing." And quoting freely from the words of St. Clare he added:

> Always keep before your eyes the point of departure, Jesus our Lord and brother. When you have reached your goal, hold on to it with tenacity; whatever you do, do it well; do not stop but rather with rapid stride and light step and such surefootedness that even the dust may not delay your forward thrust, advance with prudence and confidence, happy and eager in the way of the beatitudes (2LAg 11-13).

After all this reflection the Minister began to wonder within himself about the effects of his ministry to his brothers and sisters. Had he been effective in bringing consolation and in inspiring courage? "God alone knows really," he thought, "how helpful I have been in bringing them to a closer living of the Gospel and our Rule as members of a Eucharistic family." With his mind on these things, he came to realize how much he was now experiencing a need for consolation and encouragement. He saw perhaps more clearly than ever before that only those who know and accept their own wounds can heal and console others.

Day and night the brothers of the Province of Santiago, mainly the younger brothers, remained with the Minister in the hospital room. They consoled him with their presence and brought him bodily nourishment. They sang psalms with him and read to him spiritual and other texts. They talked to him about their vocation to follow Blessed Francis in this brotherhood. They wanted to know about his hopes, dreams, and disappointments, and they were curious to know how it was that he had left his native country in Westphalia to enter the Order.

One of the brothers who kept vigil at his bedside read to him from the Franciscan sources the passage which tells how Brother Francis once went on a pilgrimage to Santiago, and how on arriving there a serious illness laid him low, so much so that he was not

able to go to Morocco as he had intended (Fior 4; LM 9). Tradition
says that during that period he dwelt in a cabin where the friary
of the Lesser Brothers stands today. The same sources say that one
night during his illness Francis had a vision in which God revealed
to him that this brotherhood would be spread miraculously
throughout the whole world.

Another brother consoled the Minister by reading to him other
stories—how Blessed Francis once healed a crippled child who
walked with two crutches (1Cel 1); how at Cori not far from Ostia
a man who had completely lost the use of a leg was healed by
Francis who touched him with a stick marked with the Tau (3Cel
17); how even at Rome he also healed a holy woman named
Prasside, who had suffered a fall which resulted in a broken leg
and a dislocated shoulder (LM 8).

"The blind receive their sight, the lame walk" (Mt 11:5)

Towards the end of his sojourn near the tomb of the Apostle
James, Brother Hermann read in a book given him by a prelate of
the cathedral that the numerous cures attributed to the Apostle
James were not worked by all sorts of remedies, potions,
prescriptions, purgatives, ointments, and antidotes prepared by
doctors but rather solely by the grace of God granted to the Apostle.
(*Book of James* 1, C VI). This information encouraged our patient
who, in his dialogues with the brothers and several other pilgrims, learned many secrets about the spiritual journey of James,
which has fascinated countless people over the centuries. One
sentence in particular left an impression on him: "There is no need
for special reasons to follow the route of James." The journey itself
is the reason.

It is like a lifetime compressed into a few days. The journey
gives the pilgrim much more than that person would ever have to
offer. Do not look for anything special on the way to Santiago. Just
travel the road without making demands and you will receive an
abundance of wisdom, health, and interior harmony. You will be
healed and strengthened. There will be times of silence, quiet
peace, and contemplation. If the journey is what you want with all
your heart, then it becomes an attitude of mind rather than a
physical effort.

Certainly you must walk and be observant, but above all walk
with your heart. For this you must have perseverance, a readiness
to stop, listen, ponder, and contemplate. There is no need for you to

hurry. Both the crippled and the healthy can make a genuine pilgrimage to Santiago.

Many days later in his curia on the Jasmine Hill in Rome (by this time it was the holy season of Advent) the Minister heard with a special vividness the readings about the messianic era: "Strengthen the weak hands, and make firm the feeble knees. Say to those who are of fearful heart, 'Be strong, do not fear! . . . Then the eyes of the blind shall be opened, and the ears of the deaf unstopped; then the lame shall leap like a deer." (Is 35:3-4, 5-6— rephrased in Mt 11:5). He read also about Teilhard de Chardin's prayer: "May God give me the grace to hear with passion and ardor the neverending music of creation and make it audible to others."

"You have changed my lament into dance."

At the beginning of the New Year when the Minister was able to walk without the aid of crutches and when his Roman hill was redolent with the perfume of jasmine, he set out on his pilgrim way to visit the brothers and sisters of Taiwan, Hong Kong, Mozambique, Zimbabwe, and South Africa. To all he spoke about the blooming jasmine which surrounded him in Rome. He invited them to carry within their hearts the delicate flower of faith, the perfume of hope, and the sweet melody of love of life.

He used the words of St. John Chrysostom in urging the brothers and sisters, wherever he met them, towards a more profound mutual help and a universal solidarity: "Our life is a struggle. Let us therefore stand side by side and fight the same battle, remembering that all must be saved. Let us encourage those who stand solidly on their feet, those who are getting up again, and those who have fallen down" (*Gospel of John*, PG 58, 581). The Lord himself with his stick and his staff would have accompanied them along the way towards the new millennium (Ps 22:4) and changed the lament into dance, weakness into strength, lack of courage into hope. Everywhere the Minister related how Francis was not able to realize his wish to go to Morocco, but, detained in Santiago by a long illness, he was forced to return home. In particular the Minister spoke of the vision Francis had that night in Santiago according to which the Order would take root throughout the whole world and would always continue to spread.

Then he returned to his house in Rome.

Rome, March 1, 1996

1996

39. Tidings from Paraguay, Bolivia, and Chile

Background: In March 1996 the Minister General visited Paraguay, Bolivia, and Chile, affirming their evanglizing brotherhood.

"You can evangelize only what you love."

During the season of penance before Easter in the year 1996, Brother Hermann hastened on the wings of Brother Wind to three countries of South America. He had it in mind to confirm the brothers and sisters there in their service to the poor and at the same time to open himself to receive new impulses from the Gospel for his service in Rome. Everywhere he received a warm welcome— in the tropical lowlands, in the coastlands of the cool Pacific, and at the high levels where the vegetation is sparse and breathing is difficult. In all these places the brothers and sisters were sharing their experiences of crisis and hope, joy and sadness, dying out and new beginning. Everywhere they were asking one another and the Minister from Rome how they were to live and evangelize today according to the mind of Brother Francis.

In this way the discussion in Bolivia and in Paraguay turned to the manner in which the Lesser Brothers and the Jesuits had at one time attempted to evangelize the tribes of the Guaranì and the Guarayos, and how for this purpose territories were created—the so-called *reducciones*—in which the Indios formed Christian communities under the guidance of these two Orders. On this subject the Minister from Rome listened to a learned lecture in which i t was explained how the Jesuits in their *reducciones* had built the churches and houses with massive stone blocks while the Lesser Brothers used simple clay bricks. The most surprising thing, however, is that the solid walls of the Jesuits have all long disappeared whereas the miserable and rickety churches and houses of the Franciscans have remained to this day, though not without undergoing many repairs. Why? The thick stones of the sons of St. Ignatius, according to this expert in inculturation, were stolen by the rich people when the *reducciones* were dissolved and then used to build private houses and villas. These stones can still be seen today in various buildings. No one was interested in the pitiful bricks of the Lesser Brothers. So their buildings and churches have been preserved to the present.

Our man from Rome heard that there are also other differences—the Franciscans preserved the Indian names of places. The Jesuits for their part had been given a decree from their *Praepositus Generalis* (head of all the Jesuits) which obliged them to give to all their places a saint's name. At the end the Jesuits in the places where their glorious activities were located had several martyrs and confessors; some of these were also officially canonized in Rome. The Lesser Brothers in these regions, by contrast, were poor not only in their building materials but also in martyrs, and this to the present day. And the said theologian, himself a member of the Society of Jesus, concluded his exposition with these words:

> All honor to the martyrs who laid down their lives for the faith. But all honor also to those who inculturated themselves so peacefully and humbly into the peoples and cultures of the time that it was not required of them to accept martyrdom.

Brother Hermann then traveled to La Serena in northern Chile, to Santiago, and also to Santa Cruz de la Sierra and to Copacabana by Lake Titicaca with its famous sanctuary of the Virgin Mary. On the shores of these mysterious waters which are closely bound up with the mythology of Inca culture, Brother Hilarión of the tribe of the Aymara from the upper reaches of Bolivia told him about the Pachamama, the Mother Earth of the Incas. He told him as well about the condor, which is considered holy because its bold flights approach the divinity. Hilarión had been very glad to read what a German philosopher had written—that only those who know the voices and colors of Mother Earth can serve peace and reconciliation among peoples (Carl F. von Weizsäcker).

Asked what he understands by "inculturation" and what message he might have for his brothers in Latin America, the Minister recounted a parable which on this occasion he derived from his native Westphalia.

> When in our part of the world the migrating birds set out in autumn for the Mediterraneanand Africa by way of Geneva and Rome because it is getting too cold for them north of the Alps, it can be observed that they form themselves into the shape of the letter V. The scientists—they are called in

Germany "ornithologists"—have investigated this pheno-
menon, and they have discovered that the beating of a
bird's wings produces a much greater force of propulsion
than the bird needs. It can therefore pass some of this on to
its neighbors. Birds of migration flying south in V-
formation have available 71% more energy than those
which fly alone.

Using this example, our visitor made clear that the brothers
and sisters of St. Clare and St. Francis in Latin America must
likewise learn to overcome "forms of personal and collective
individualism" and develop a "new culture of solidarity with each
other and with the poor," They should cooperate more in order to
strengthen one another and together discover new horizons. They
must be bold and contemplative like the condor but at the same
time poor, missionary, and in solidarity like ordinary birds of
passage. Indeed, he commended the birds of passage and their
manner of movement as a parable of a Church truly fraternal and in
solidarity. At the conclusion of his conversations with the
Apostolic Prefects (heads of mission areas) of El Beni, Nuflo de
Chávez, and Cuevo and their missionaries, the Minister recalled to
the mind of all: "We can only truly evangelize and can only
inculturate ourselves into what we really love." Then he moved on.

"Eyes which are clear and always remain young"

In Santiago, Chile, and in Cochabamba, Bolivia, Brother
Hermann had the privilege of receiving the profession of ten young
brothers into the fraternity. The songs and the melodies of the
instruments of the Cordillera of the Andes, the Andean flute and
the charango, sounded for a long time in the mild evening air and
were carried out into the rugged mountain valleys and into the
barrios of the poor. These were celebrations of life and hope for the
whole Order and for the People of God who had gathered in great
crowds from as far away as Sucre, Potosì, and Oruro.

In his homily the Minister called upon all the young brothers
of the continent to rejoice in their lowly mission as brothers of the
Poverello of Assisi. They ought to entrust themselves to the
mystery of the living God who loves the earth and its little ones.
The well-known Chilean poetess Gabriella Mistral, a member of
the Secular Franciscan Order, representing all *minores* said: "If

you, my God, look upon me, then do I become beautiful." Then in his own words the Minister continued:

Never let your hopes become cold,
    but follow the inspiration of your boldest dreams.
The seed of hope was implanted deep in your heart:
    let it grow in patience and joyfulness,
Let it come to maturity and bear fruit.
For it can be harvested only by one who is long in breath.
One who is impatient, on the other hand,
    will give up in disappointment.
God is in the midst of your life, in your darkness,
    in your light, on the summits of your majestic hills,
    in the upper lands and in the valleys.
Give him your trust; always count on him.
He himself will strengthen you,
    he will give you the wings of a bird of passage
    and perhaps the pinions of the condor.
All that is truly great is not complicated but simple.
Do not be afraid to turn your heart and eye
    to the impossible.
For only in that way will what is possible become reality.

And he concluded by encouraging all the brothers and sisters of the continent, and even himself, with the words of a European, Soren Kierkegaard:

If I were offered the fulfillment of a wish,
    then I would want to have neither riches nor power,
    but a passion for the possible.
I would want eyes which remain young forever
    always alight with the longing
    to discover what is possible.

Shortly before Palm Sunday, Brother Hermann set out on his return journey from the Pacific coast by Antofagasta and Valparaiso, from the Cordillera of the Andes, from the uplands by La Paz and Copacabanca at Lake Titicaca, the highest lake in the world, where in accordance with an old custom he had been clothed with the protective coat of the Madonna of the Poor. From the former *reducciones* and present houses of his brothers around La Paz, Cochabamba, Santa Cruz, and Asunción, he returned to Rome, to his modest hill not far from the Vatican. There winter was not

yet quite past, and the yellow jasmine, an advance messenger of
paschal confidence, had just begun timidly to show its blossom.

Rome, May 1, 1996

40. A prayer for the Americas

Background: In May 1995 the Plenary Council of the Order met in
Malta to discuss the proposed Ratio Evangelisationis *(Plan for
Evangelization).* That text included the following prayer,
composed in 1991 by Brother Hermann Schalück.

Mary,
Mother of our Brother and Lord Jesus Christ,
  poor and crucified,
Mother of our Family, Mother of the poor,
  hear our confident supplication,
  which we address to you today.
So many people in the world
  lack material and spiritual bread;
So many minds and so many hearts
  lack the bread of truth and of love;
So many peoples
  lack the bread of the Word and of the Eucharist.
Root out from the hearts of so many men and women
  the selfishness which impoverishes.
May the peoples of the Americas
  and of the whole world know how to accept
  the true Light, walking along the paths
  of Peace and Justice,
  in mutual respect and in a solidarity
  rooted in the humanity of our God.
Our Lady of the Portiuncula, brown Lady of the Americas,
  enlighten our hope,
  purify our eyes and our hearts,
  accompany us along the paths
  of the new evangelization,
  towards a world ever more just and free for all. Amen.

41. "The Lord disciplines those he loves" (Heb 12:6)

In the heat of the Roman summer of 1996, the fifth of his time as Minister, Brother Hermann felt an urgent need to take some time for repose after his many journeys to the four corners of the earth and in the face of many an "infirmity and distress" *(Canticle of the Creatures)*. And so he retired to the green forests of his native Westphalia to allow his soul to breathe freely. He gratefully remembered the many encounters with brothers and sisters, encounters which had been for him a great encouragement, but he also reflected before God on why so many things had seemed to him "unbearably bitter" *(Testament)*. He asked an older brother how it might be possible to find his way back to inner peace and "sweetness in body and soul" *(Testament)*. The latter quoted a saying from the Middle Kingdom: "You cannot prevent the birds of anxiety and care from flying over your head. But you can prevent them from building nests in your hair."

Then mindful of what was said by St. John Chrysostom, the Minister also asked a Sister of St. Clare for her advice. For this great Father of the Church once wrote: "Indeed women are often the right spiritual teachers for men. Men are often like crows scratching around in the dust and smoke, while women are able to rise up like eagles to higher and lighter spheres." This sister advised him to listen attentively to the voice of God in creation, in Scripture, in his own life, "for God has given us only one mouth but two ears."

Finally the Minister encountered a brother from Islam who comforted him with the wisdom from the tradition of the Sufis:

If you want to overcome cares of all kinds, anxieties, disappointments and stress, and to prevent what is dark in you from becoming stronger than what is light, then you must behave as did the wise man whom I met in an oasis of the Arabian desert. While he was under a palm tree enjoying his midday nap, a monkey threw a heavy coconut with great force onto his head. He lay there for a long time as though senseless. Then for a long while he fiendishly planned in his mind just how he would saw down the tree and chase the monkey in order to punish him. When finally he recovered his calm in prayer, he resolved to act quite differently. The Sufi searched for the coconut and lifted it up out of the sand, contemplated it and stroked it as a gift from God. He cracked it open and drank its milk, for he was indeed thirsty. He ate the tasty flesh of the fruit, for he had become aware how hungry he was. Out of one half of the shell he made himself a protective helmet against any future attacks and against the burning sun. The other half he began using to scoop up water for his inner and outer refreshment.

Finally, in an anonymous author of the fifteenth century the Minister read: "Sometimes we need games and other pleasant forms of madness if we want to remain sane."

Then the feast of the Portiuncula approached, and as usual the Minister hurried to that holy spot in Umbria where the Order of St. Francis and St. Clare had found its origin. This time he prayed particularly for peace and reconciliation in the world and in the Church of Christ but also in his own heart. He realized with a new clarity that from this "small portion" of the earth great impulses and hopes have kept going out for the Church, for the world, for his brothers and sisters, for himself. Together with the two thousand young pilgrims whom he met on August 2 in the piazza in front of the basilica, he prayed that the Church and the Franciscan family might always receive the gift of new poets and prophets. And he asked for himself and for his brothers and sisters true fruits of the Spirit—joy in contemplation, selflessness, a sense of humor, creativity, patience with oneself, acknowledgment of one's own limitations, trust in the Spirit of God in creation, in the Church, in one's own fraternity. And together they sang this song:

> Brother Francis, you are as transparent as water.
> You are as bright as the spark carried aloft by the wind.
> You proclaim peace in our hearts and in our streets.
> You are for all people and for the groaning creation
>   an instrument of peace.
> Brother Francis, go with us on the road of the
>   freedom of the children of God."

At the end he blessed all those who had gathered at the Portiuncula with the words:

> The Lord bless you.
> May he fill your feet with dance and
>   your arms with strength.
> May he fill your hearts with tenderness and
>   your eyes with laughter.

May he fill your ears with music and
    your nose with pleasant scents.
May he fill your mouth with jubilation and
    your heart with joy.
May he give us ever anew the desert graces:
    silence, fresh water, and renewed hope.
May he give us all ever anew the strength
    to give hope a new face.
May the Lord bless you.

After that the Minister did not return to Rome, to his hill on which flowers the jasmine. Instead, with new courage and inner refreshment he undertook a journey to the regions of the Zambezi and Congo Rivers in Africa, in order to visit his brothers and sisters in those areas, to strengthen them in the following of Christ and to receive from them new impulses for his own service. In Zaire he had the joy of receiving into the Order a large number of young brothers as they made their profession, as had happened not so long before in Jangamo in Mozambique, in Pacet in distant Indonesia, as also in Cochabamba in Bolivia, and in Chile. He experienced in his own person how good the Lord is and how he himself wills to build up our fraternity ever anew. Neither did he ever again forget that the Lord often disciplines especially those whom he loves (cf. Heb 12:6).

42. On the Minister's journey to Zaire

From Tiber to Congo River

After the feast of Portiuncula in 1996, Brother Hermann and Brother Peter flew from the city of Rome, which is washed by the Tiber, to the city of Kinshasa, situated on the banks of the Congo River, to visit the Brothers and Sisters of Zaire. On arrival at the capital of Zaire, they continued their journey to Bukavu and Goma, situated on the shores of Lake Kivu close to the frontier with Rwanda. Here the green pastures were dotted with white army tents full of refugees. Then they went to Mbuyi-Mai, a city of diamond mines. On a hill nearby can be seen the poor dwellings which house the various branches of the Franciscan family.

Next they went to Lubumbashi, Katanga that was, and from there to Kamina, a town in which brothers from Flanders began the work of evangelization seventy years ago. The Minister and his companion arrived in a small plane belonging to an Adventist missionary who prayed with his passengers before takeoff and then flew them to Kolwezi. Finally they arrived back in Lubumbashi by car and flew from there to Kinshasa. Brother Hermann and his companion were received everywhere with the following words of African welcome: "The visitor is like a cloud which, even though it may pass quickly, is always a blessing from God, for it never departs without having moistened our dry earth."

Brothers and Sisters of the People

In Lubumbashi twelve novices from the friary at Lukafu made their temporary profession into the hands of the Minister to the sounds of the tam-tam and the joyful exclamations of the People of God. During a Mass in Mbuyi-Mai, celebrated on the eve of the feast of St. Clare beneath the shade of a giant mango tree in the garden of the Poor Ladies, members of the Secular Franciscan Order presented Brother Hermann with a *kiombo*, a piece of heavy iron which in ancient times was used as a marriage dowry and also as a means of payment in the slave market, a *kapudi* or kind of whistle used to announced the arrival of a tribal chief in a village and also used to signal the beginning and end of a hunt, and a wooden vase which had belonged to a tribal chief. In the church of Kamina, an elderly catechist exhibited a portrait of the Minister, painted from a photograph. When he presented it to the Minister later on, the latter was pleasantly surprised to find himself portrayed as an African.

In the cloister of the friary in Kolwezi, he saw a donkey, a sheep and a marabou walking along together in peace and harmony. There also six friars made their solemn profession into the hands of the Minister from Rome. The cathedral was packed with God's people. The bishop kneeling at his prie-dieu was praying for the Lesser Brothers. The air vibrated with melodies and rhythms little known in Rome. The rows of people shook and danced flamenco-style to the roll of drums, the rhythm of the dance, and the clapping of hands. This feast lasted three hours.

In his homily the Minister expressed the gratitude of the whole brotherhood to the Lord, seeing that buds and shoots continued to sprout from the ancient trunk of the Order, notwithstanding some dried up branches. He spoke of silence and contemplation from which flow the real strength to strive and to resist. He encouraged each one to live out the charism of *minority* and of the *family spirit* that makes us members of the one family of Jesus, a spirit stronger than the differences of tribe and language, without at the same time ceasing to be sons and daughters of the people to whom we belong. This is the special gift which Franciscans have to offer to the African continent. He went on to say that our God desires that people live in freedom and that creation should thrive. We must, therefore, be open to the dream of justice and peace, for the person who does not dream becomes old before his time, and the African brothers are called upon to present a youthful visage to the Order and the Church.

Signs of Peace and of Hope

In the course of a celebration in Kinshasa with the Franciscan family, the group placed on the Minister a mantle of yellow wool. They decked him out in peacock feathers and painted his arms with pure white chalk, signs of the dignity and authority of a chief. Immediately the Minister took his seat in the center and invited all to give witness and to proclaim by word and deed, as authentic brothers and sisters of Francis in Africa, hope, peace, and life wherever they encounter poverty or lack of liberty. And he reminded all, in the words of Martin Luther King, Jr.:

> If you cannot be a spruce tree on the top of a high mountain,
>   be at least a fertile blade of grass in the valley.
> If you cannot be an oak tree, at least be a shrub.
> If you are not a highway, be at least a viable pathway.
> If you cannot be the sun, try to be a small star.
> Endeavor to find out the secret plan that should
>   structure your life, and adopt it as a practice.

Then Brother Hermann added that the task of Franciscan brothers and sisters wherever they live and *evangelize* is that of reuniting the scattered, healing the broken, binding up wounds, feeding the hungry, drying the tears of those who weep, and consoling those who are lonely.

Return and Farewell

During another gathering with sisters and brothers in Kinshasa, something never before experienced in the Order occurred—the Minister sent forth an African brother to the missions. The name of this first Franciscan African missionary is

Joseph Kanyinda, who was sent to collaborate in the implantation of the Fraternity in the Central African Republic. The whole assembly gave thanks to God for this sign of life, of increase, and of hope. When they bade goodbye to the Minister and his companion, the brothers and sisters sang this song composed by a Christian from Zaire:

Lord, help us to build up a new world,
  one in which the lion will heal the wounds of the lamb,
  and the serpent dry the tears of the infant.
Help us to build up a world in which
  a little girl will caress the lion's mane,
  and the leopard and a man will hold hand and paw,
  together proclaiming peace.
Lord, when the serpent injects his poison,
  make me honey from the coconut to counteract it.
When an earthquake opens the ground,
  make of me a bamboo ladder stretching like a bridge
  to unite the ledges of the abyss.
When people are invaded by waves of doubt and anguish,
  make of me a safe ship in which to cross the torrent.

Jasmine and Pomegranates

In due course Brother Hermann began his journey back to his own hill on which flowers the jasmine. On his arrival he planted a pomegranate *(punica granatum)* which the Africans regard as a symbol of fruitful motherhood. Its fruit, according to the Fathers of the Church, is an image of the mystery of the Church. Just as the pomegranate gathers together in harmonious array beneath its skin so many shining, juicy seeds, so the Church unites so many tribes and so many different peoples in the unity of one faith,